REUPHOLSTERING AT HOME

A DO-IT-YOURSELF MANUAL FOR TURNING OLD FURNITURE INTO NEW SHOWPIECES

REUPHOLSTERING AT HOME

A DO-IT-YOURSELF MANUAL FOR TURNING OLD FURNITURE INTO NEW SHOWPIECES

PETER NESOVICH

Crown Publishers, Inc.   New York

All diagrams in this book were done by Leonard Contillo, Jr., and all
photographs and yardage estimate charts were taken by the author.
All pieces in the yardage estimate charts were upholstered by
the author.

Inquiries should be addressed to Crown Publishers, Inc., One Park Avenue,
New York, N.Y. 10016

Printed in the United States of America
Published simultaneously in Canada by
General Publishing Company Limited

Library of Congress Cataloging in Publication Data

Nesovich, Peter.
Reupholstering at home.

1. Upholstery. I. Title.
TT198.N44   1979   684.1'2   79-12449
ISBN: 0-517-538180 (cloth)
0-517-538199 (paper)

10   9   8   7   6   5   4   3

ACKNOWLEDGMENTS

I would like to thank my children, Peter, Nelly Dorwart, and Monika Contillo, my wife, Paula, Jeff Dorwart, and Lenny Contillo for their help and support of my book.

I would like to thank the New England Upholstery Supply Co. for their expert advice on upholstery fabrics and supplies.

Finally, I would like to thank my many students who have given me inspiration and encouragement along the way.

CONTENTS

INTRODUCTION

Have you ever wanted to recover an old piece of furniture but like many people did not know where to begin or were frightened by the enormity of the task? If so, this book is for you.

This book is the product of my many years of experience. It is a step-by-step illustrated manual designed to teach the novice to transform an old piece of furniture into a showpiece. I will outline the procedures for reupholstering different styles of furniture and at the same time share with you all the shortcuts I have found that can simplify the project.

Reupholstering requires minimal space, a few simple tools, and a creative desire. You need not be a woodcraftsman, as there are many places you can find an old frame suitable for your needs. The cost is virtually limited to the fabric.

The greatest incentive is the self-satisfaction of saying ''I did it myself'' repeated every time someone comments on your new furniture.

Can you do it? Of course you can! All you need is a little ambition and confidence in yourself.

TOOLS

An upholsterer needs special tools. A large upholstery shop will naturally have a variety of tools but you at home will need only a few, some of which you may already have. Buy the best tools you can afford. Supply sources include large department stores and upholstery supply shops, and either can be consulted for advice.

Let us first examine the tools you must have (see illustration 1).

(a) Scissors: Without scissors it is impossible to complete any upholstery project. What is important is the size and sharpness. Good sizes are 9″ and 10″, heavy duty and sharp to give a perfect cut.

(b) Hammer: A hammer's chief use is for driving in tacks and nails. A magnetized tack hammer is used mostly in upholstery. One end is magnetized to pick up tacks; the other end to drive in tacks. However, perfect jobs have been completed with an ordinary carpenter's hammer.

(c) Staple remover: One of the best tools for removing staples and tacks is Berry's Staple Remover. Courtesy Berry's Limited, P.O. Box 6414, Lubbock, Texas 79413.

(d) Tack puller tool: An alternative to a staple remover is a claw tool for removing tacks.

(e) Claw tool: Narrow at the point to get under heads of ornamental nails and tacks without harming fabric or wood.

(f) Webbing stretcher: This is used to pull the webbing tight. It is inexpensive and well worth the job it does.

(g) Stretching tool: This is used to pull steel webbing tight.

(h) **Tufting needle:** Time Saver Hollow Upholstery Needle with Tufting Clasp. This new revolutionary-type needle with attached tufting clasp is indeed a time-saver for the upholstery industry. An excellent tool for putting on buttons. The needle is 14″ in length.

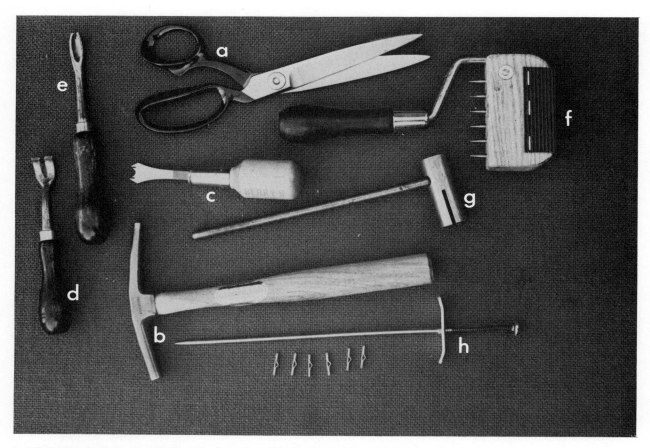

1. **Upholsterer's tools. Tools a, b, d, e, f, and h are C. S. Osborne & Co. tools and are sold through upholstery supply distributors.**

Other tools you will need:

(i) *Tape measure:* A flexible tape measure is needed for taking measurements on furniture.

(j) *Yardstick:* This is used to measure the fabric and as a straightedge for marking cutting and sewing lines.

(k) *Sewing needle:* A regular sewing needle is used sometimes to sew the outside cover, part of the wings, and for general use.

(l) *Curved 4″ needle:* This is for sewing the outside covers and for general use.

(m) **Straight 8″ needle:**   Used for attaching springs to the webbing, putting on buttons, and general use.

(n) **Pins:**   Eye or T-form pins are used to secure the covers for fitting and sewing.

(o) **Chalk:**   White or tailor's chalk is needed to mark cutting and sewing lines. Use washable chalk.

(p) **Heavy-duty staple gun:**   This is a handy, timesaving tool. It is used for tacking on dust covers, panels, and welting cord. If you are going to do a lot of upholstering, buy one. Useful staple sizes are 5/16″, 3/8″, and 1/2″.

(q) **Screwdrivers, wrenches, and pliers:**   These tools are necessary for chairs and couches that must be taken apart for reupholstering.

(r) **Sewing machine:**   A home-type sewing machine will do the job for you but use a #14 or #16 needle, and purchase a zipper-foot attachment (see illustration 16).

MATERIALS

Upholstery materials may be purchased in department stores but in some cases the materials you need can be found only in upholstery shops. If you have a problem, go to your nearest upholstery shop.

Let us look at the necessary materials for the home upholsterer:

(a) **Upholstery fabric:**   This is the most costly item as well as the most important; it must be durable and decorative. It is available in many patterns and materials to fit all needs and tastes.

(b) **Sewing thread:**   Use any heavy-duty thread—cotton or polyester. The most important thing is to match the thread to the fabric by weight and color. Most upholsterers use cotton #24–4 or nylon #B69.

(c) **Sewing twine (tufting twine):**   This is for sewing on buttons, for tufting, and for attaching springs to the webbing.

(d) **Welting cord:**   A piece of furniture is dressed up with welting cord.

(e) **Tacks:**   These are short nails with a sharp point and a relatively large flat head. Sizes #1 to #24 are available but the most useful sizes are #3, #4, #6, and #12, depending upon the thickness of the material to be tacked.

(f) **Tacking tape:**   Hard paper (chipboard) used to attach panels in blind tacking. The best width to use is 1/2″.

(g) **Cambric:**   A close-woven, medium heavy material, black or gray in color, used to cover chair and sofa bottoms. Also called dustcloth.

(h)   Metal tacking strip: 24″ and 30″ long used to blind-tack the back panel and other panels of furniture. It makes the finishing smooth and saves you time. Without this, you must sew the material by hand (see illustration 33).

Certain jobs will require some of these materials:

(i)   Spring twine: Used for tying springs to the frame and together for support (see illustrations 64–71).

(j)   Nails for spring twine and steel webbing: Similar to plasterboard nails but with sturdier heads. Do not use plasterboard nails. These nails are grooved to prevent backing out.

(k)   Steel webbing: Steel webbing with stretching tool and nails are shown in illustration 2. Nailing steel webbing over old webbing forces the springs into place. If old jute webbing is good but sags down you may use steel webbing. In other cases it is better to replace old webbing with new webbing.

(l)   Burlap: A cloth 40″ wide made of jute flax or hemp to cover the springs.

(m)   Jute webbing: A strong fabric of cotton or other material woven in 4″ wide strips. It is used for supporting the seats of stuffed chairs or sofas, also for the arms and backs of some pieces of furniture. Use regular for arms and backs, heavy duty for seats (see illustrations 56 and 57).

(n)   Frame edging: A roll of paper, straw, hair, moss, or other material covered with muslin or burlap. It is used on the edge of springs and on wooden frame edges of chairs or sofas to make the edges soft and round (see illustrations 74–77).

(o)   Cotton: 27″ wide, 3/4″ or 1″ thick, it is used for all padding needs.

(p)   Foam rubber or polyfoam: It has a variety of uses and comes in many sizes.

(q)   Muslin: 40″ wide thin cotton cloth of plain weave is used to cover the padding.

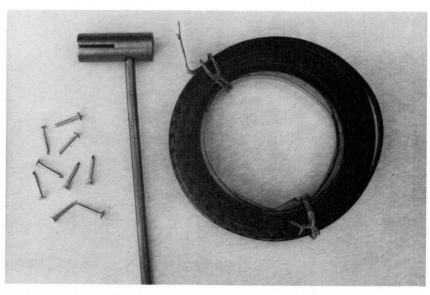

2.   **Steel webbing, including stretching tool and nails. Flat Band Stretcher courtesy of Neversag Products, Inc.**

(r)   Gimp: Used on many old-fashioned pieces of furniture, or for that old-fashioned look. It is for finishing the upholstery edge of panels. It comes in 1/2″ width and a choice of rich colors (see illustration 21).

(s)   Double welting cord: This is used on modern furniture to finish the upholstery edge instead of gimp (see illustration 20).

(t)   Trim or decorative nails: Used on old-fashioned furniture for the finishing edge (see illustrations 132 and 133).

(u)   Rubber cement: Used to glue pieces of foam rubber or polyfoam together. No substitutes.

(v)   Fabric glue: Used to glue on gimp, double cording, and other materials.

FABRIC SELECTION

When planning to recover a piece of furniture, the first thing you will want to do is to look at upholstery fabrics. Fabrics come in many colors, patterns, and textures.

You should buy good quality fabric with a nice design and color to match the rest of your decor. Since there are hundreds of material patterns, you can easily get lost in the selection. Take the time to look in different material shops.

If you are a novice at selecting material, it is imperative that you consult fabric experts and pay special attention to labels. The look and feel of a fabric may make you think it is good but it may not be so. For the best results take sample books home and sit and look through them with your family, friends, and relatives. By examining several patterns and colors and comparing them with your room colors, you will find the perfect fabric.

3.   Selecting the fabric.

Fabric selection requires knowing certain factors:

(a)   Width: 54" is the most economical size for upholstery, since with this dimension the cutting waste is minimal.

(b)   Pattern: The pattern size is very important, and a repeating pattern varies from a few inches up to 28″. For small pieces of furniture use small patterns, while large furniture can be upholstered with big patterns.

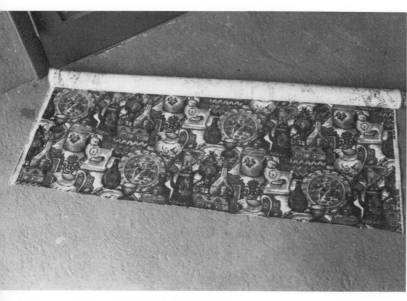

About 90 percent of all fabric is laid out with the pattern running like wallpaper—running the width of the fabric (side to side). See illustration 4. About 10 percent is "railroaded"; that is, it is printed with the pattern running the length of the fabric (parallel with the selvage edges). See illustration 5. For large pieces of furniture, for example a sofa, select a fabric that can be laid in any direction, or railroaded. Railroading is necessary for long pieces of furniture when unpieced panels are needed.

5.   Railroaded print.

4.   Normal 54″ width print.

(c) Velvet: Velvet is a very difficult material with which to work. The material appears in different shades as you look at it from different angles. Because of this, it is difficult to recover a piece of furniture to make all the panels look the same. Velvet, however, is not recommended for railroading, since it has a definite up and down in the way the nap lies.

(d) Striped fabric: When covering a piece of furniture, vertical stripes look best (see illustration 6). Most stripes run the length of the material, parallel with the selvage edges. This type of fabric is not railroaded (see illustration 7). Some materials have stripes running side to side, also called railroaded material (see illustration 8).

For welting, striped material should be cut on the bias, or pick out one stripe color and make the welting that color.

6. Stripes running vertical.

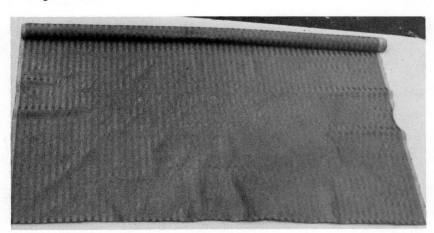

7. Stripes running the length of the material.

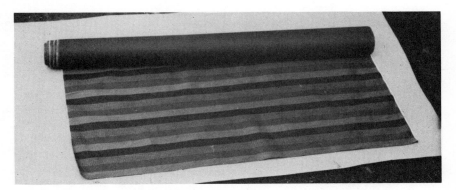

8. Stripes running side to side.

(e) Yardage estimates: It is very difficult to estimate exactly how many yards of material you will need for your job as different sizes and styles of furniture require different amounts. However, a rough guide is that a standard size 72″ long sofa with two or three cushions will take approximately 10 yards then, add 1 1/2 yards for the skirt if you wish to put one on. A standard club chair with cushion will require about 5 yards and add 1 yard for skirt if you wish to put one on. From this point you may estimate approximately how many yards you will need for a smaller or larger size chair or sofa. Check with a yardage chart and compare.

YARDAGE ESTIMATOR

The figures represent the approximate yards of 54″ material needed to reupholster the type of furniture shown. The oversized (over 6 feet long) sofas are marked with an L, followed by the length of each in feet.

27" X 41", H-18"

3/4

5

5

3

5

3/4

3/4

3/4

6

3

1

5

6

3/4

2

2

3

3

4

4

3/4

3/4

1/2

2 ½

1 CHAIR - 3/4 YD. 2 CHAIRS - 1 YD.

3

1¼

3

5

5

5

2½

5

6

12

10

11

2

3

10

18 L-8

6

12 L-7

4 PC. SET 21 YD.

MEASUREMENT AND CUTTING

The final upholstery fabric is the most costly item you will have to buy as well as the most important. Therefore, to save costly miscuts, much attention must be paid to the layout and correct measurements. My rule is "Take seven measurements for one cut." Then you will be sure of your measurements before you cut and will eliminate costly errors. Some other rules to follow are listed below.

1.   Before marking the panels, you must make the final decision as to which direction the weave lines or pattern is to run on your chair or sofa. Remember that most fabrics are made to run in any direction, but some can run in only one as there is a top and bottom to the pattern.

9.   **Pattern with a top and bottom.**

10.   **Patterns without a top and bottom. Patterns copyrighted by Quaker Fabric Corporation.**

2.   The direction in which the weave lines run, stripes or any pattern, must be placed in this manner: all horizontal panels must be placed running from the front to the back. All vertical panels must be placed running from the bottom to the top (see illustration 13).

3.   When cutting velvet and other shiny materials, care must be taken so that all shading on covered panels will be the same. To avoid mistakes remember that on all horizontal panels the nap is laid from the back to the front, and verticals are laid from the bottom to the top (see illustration 14).

4.   All upholstery must be put on symmetrically, that is, you must center the pattern (see illustration 15).

5.   The most economical method for cutting the fabric is to mark all the panels needed for the job in rectangular form on a piece of paper. This is called a paper plan. This plan should show the direction the fabric will lie on your furniture, the dimensions, and the location code.

PAPER PLAN (Example)

Location Code

S—Seat	CF—Cushion Facing
A—Inside Arm	W—Inside Wing
B—Inside Back	OW—Outside Wing
BX—Boxing	OA—Outside Arm
BR—Border	OB—Outside Back
ZBX—Zipper Boxing	CR—Cording

Note: The arrows show the direction the fabric will lie on the furniture and X and Y are your dimensions. Measurements taken for each piece of furniture are given in the working pages.

6.   On the finishing side of the fabric, mark the pieces in chalk. First work with the large pieces and then mark the small pieces in between. After marking a few panels, cut them out, then on the reverse side mark on tape stuck to the fabric the names of the panels by code and arrows indicating the direction the panel will lie on the furniture. Repeat the process.

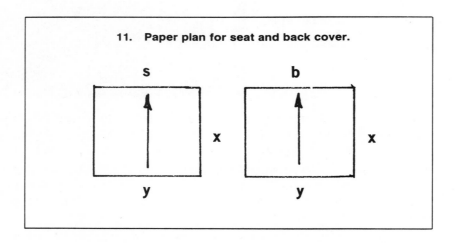

11.   **Paper plan for seat and back cover.**

FRAME

The frame is the foundation unit of a piece of furniture. It has a great deal to do with the price and structure of the piece of furniture. The thing to remember is that a sturdy old frame is better than a weak new one. Old, already upholstered frames that need only reupholstering can be purchased or obtained from many sources.

You may be given a piece of furniture from someone who is moving out of the neighborhood. There is always a chair or sofa at a garage or yard sale that could be reupholstered or, even better, your local used furniture store would definitely have something you would enjoy working on.

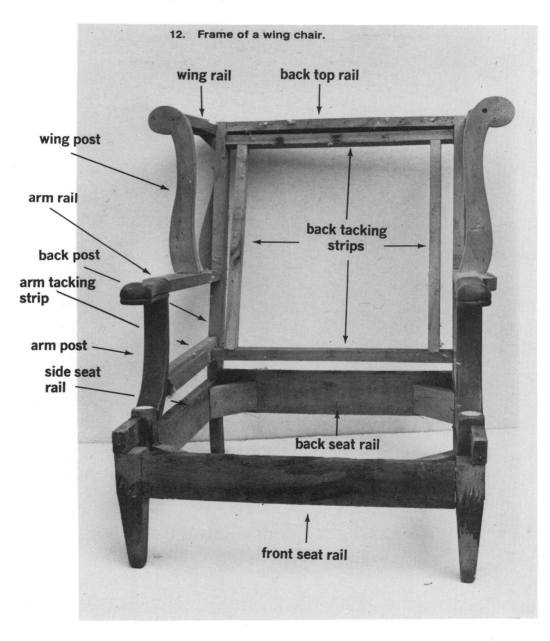

12. Frame of a wing chair.

wing rail

back top rail

wing post

arm rail

back post

arm tacking strip

arm post

side seat rail

back tacking strips

back seat rail

front seat rail

PANELING

We panel a room when we remodel a house to improve the looks of the interior. We also use paneling in upholstery to improve the looks of furniture, from old to new.

By putting new fabric on furniture, following the direction as shown in the illustration with each panel centered, you improve not only the furniture but the whole character of the room.

You must be sure each panel is placed in the right direction and the pattern centered.

13.   Arrows show the direction the pattern should lie.

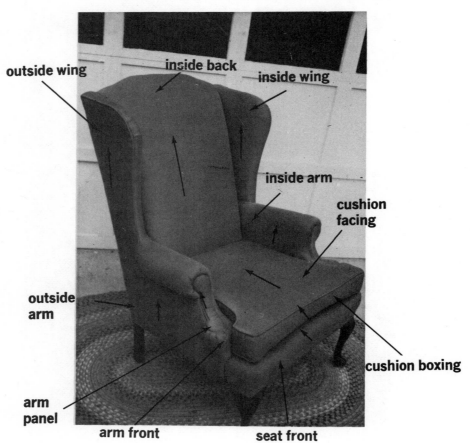

outside wing

inside back

inside wing

inside arm

cushion facing

outside arm

cushion boxing

arm panel

arm front

seat front

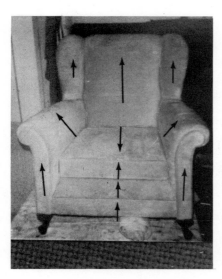

14. Arrows show the direction the nap should lie for velvet.

15. Centered pattern.

SEWING MACHINES

When the sewing machine was invented over a hundred years ago many people could not believe that it could sew. So it may be the same with you when I tell you that you can use your domestic sewing machine for upholstering. All you need is a few inexpensive accessories that I will mention, and some simple modifications. Most important, you must take care of your machine by keeping it well oiled and all parts properly maintained.

Industrial upholstering machines have advantages in their higher frames and are more solidly constructed than machines for household use but a domestic machine will do the same job.

To sew with ease on your sewing machine it is essential to pay particular attention to a few requirements:

1. The sewing machine should be set according to your manual for the fabric that is being sewn, such as: thread tension and foot pressure (models vary). Therefore, your instruction book should be consulted.

2. The size of the needle should conform to the size of the thread, and both should be suitable to the material. A #16 needle should be used for sewing upholstery fabric.

3. Top and bottom threads must be the same color and strength. Use a color thread to match your upholstery fabric.

4. For maximum strength, use a narrow stitch. Narrow stitches make a seam stronger and hide the thread better.

5. Use your zipper-foot attachment for many jobs such as welting cording, installing the zipper, and so on.

6. Use the very narrow sewing foot attachment for sewing channels in upholstery covering.

With practice, you can sew your upholstery fabric with the same ease that you sew a dress.

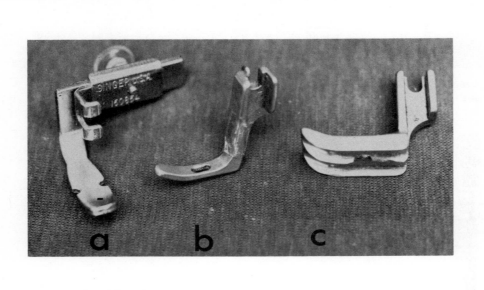

16. Pressure foot attachments.
a. Zipper Foot
b. Narrow Foot
c. Double Cording Foot

Note: Do not leave any upholstery material near the electric bulb on your machine for any length of time, especially synthetic material that hardens and changes color due to melting of the material.

BASIC UPHOLSTERY WORK

Before a carpenter can build a house, there are some basic things about carpentry he must know if he is to have any chance for success. So it is with reupholstery.

The following are some basics:

SINGLE WELTING CORD

Welt is a strip of material you fold over a cord and stitch to it, using a zipper foot on your sewing machine.

Welting cord is decorative and gives a tailored appearance to an upholstered piece of furniture. It is usually made of the same fabric as the chair or sofa but can be different for accentuation.

Bias-cut striped material for welting cord or cut it from one color stripe that is the best looking. Velvet should also be bias-cut, and while it makes no difference on other material, all welting strips should be cut in the same direction on the fabric.

17.   Striped material.

18.   Strips for welting cord of striped material.
    a. Bias Cut
    b. Cut from One Color
    c. Cross Cut

Welting cord should be made the following way: first cut a 2″ wide strip of the upholstery material as long as needed for your measurements. If you cannot make it from one piece, cut more and sew them together with a 1/2″ seam. Next fold the material around the cord and sew close to the cord, using a zipper-foot attachment on your sewing machine.

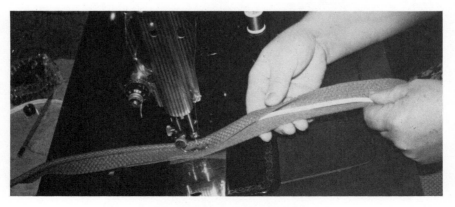

19.   Making welting cord.

DOUBLE WELTING CORD

Double welting cord is used on newer pieces of furniture where the finishing wood shows as in illustration 20. It is decorative and takes the place of gimp, which is used on old-fashioned furniture (see illustration 21). Double welting cord finishes off the upholstery edge on the wooden frame.

20.   Upholstery edge finished with double cording.

21.   Upholstery edge finished with gimp.

22.   Strip of material for double cording.

The double welting cord is made the following way:

1. Cut a strip of the upholstery material 2″ wide and the length required. Again, piecing can be done as for single welting cord.

2. On the wrong side of the strip, lay the double cording flush to one side of the strip and sew down the center line of the double cording from beginning to end.

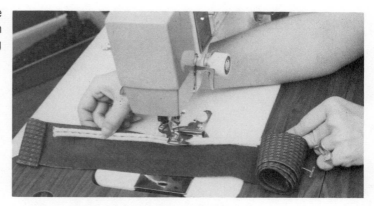

23.   Sewing the double cording to the strip.

3. Next fold the strip over the cord twice and then sew down the center of the cording to the end.

24.   Finishing sewing the double cording.

4. Trim the excess strip close to the seam.

25.   Trimming the double-cording excess.

26. **Border on the seat of a chair.**

BORDERS

A border is a narrow strip of upholstery material, with or without a welt, which is blind-tacked or sewed on one side and the other side tacked to the frame. Borders are used for finishing trims on the seat, arms, or back of some chairs or sofas. They give the furniture a more finished look and dress it up.

Making borders without welting cord:

1. Cut a strip of upholstery material to the right dimensions, remembering to match up stripes or patterns with adjoining panels.

2. Blind-tack one side (a), and tack the other side (b) to the frame as in illustration 28.

3. Tack the ends of the border (c).

Tack the ends of the border (c) in front for furniture with arm panels and on the side for furniture without panels.

27. **Double border on the back of a chair.**

28. **Blind-tacked border without a welting cord.**

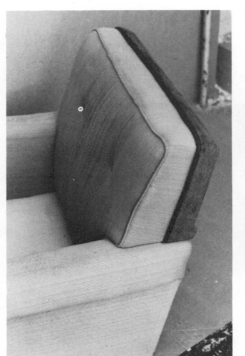

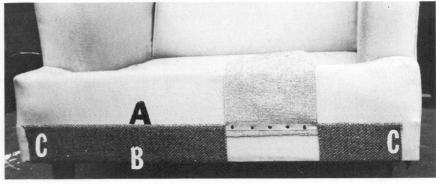

Making borders with welting cord:

1. Cut a strip of upholstery material to the right dimension, remembering to match up stripes or pattern with adjoining panels.

2. Make separate cording the same length as your border.

3. Sew the cording to the border strip as in illustration 29.

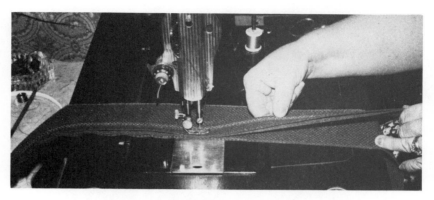

29. Sewing the welting cord to the border strip.

4. Blind-tack the side where the cording is installed (a), and tack the other side (b) to the frame as in illustration 30.

5. Tack the ends of the border (c).

30. Blind-tacked border with a welting cord.

Tack the ends of the border (c) in front for furniture with arm panels and on the side for furniture without panels.

BOXING

Boxing is a strip of upholstery material, with or without a welting cord, which is sewn to the larger pieces on both sides.

Boxings are used on most cushions and on the arms or backs of some chairs or sofas. It gives the furniture not only a dressy look but is necessary to completely finish that part of the project. Boxing with welting cord gives a more dressy look.

Complete information is given in Step 13, "The Cushion."

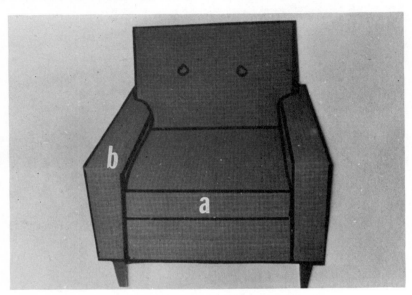

31. Chair with boxing on the cushion (a) and on the arm (b).

BLIND STITCHING

Blind stitching is a technique for making the stitches hold a seam together invisibly. They are hand-sewn stitches that are used to join cover sections at edges that cannot be machine sewn or tacked in place. Blind stitches are usually used on corners and edges. A 3″ curved needle or straight needle is required to make a blind stitch. Use color of thread to match the cover.

BLIND TACKING

Blind tacking is a technique to install edges of some cover section to the frame by using tacking tape (cardboard strip) or metal tacking strip to produce invisibly tacked edges. It will hide the tacks, staples, and edges. For blind tacking with tacking tape, you place the cover at the rail with a few tacks, inside out and upside down, then tack tacking tape over the panel edge, spacing the tacks every inch or less.

To blind-tack sides of panel, use a metal tacking strip.

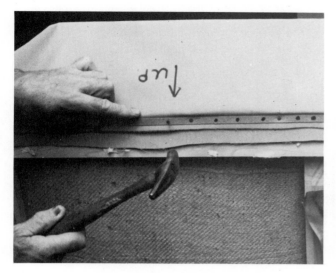

32.   Blind tacking with tacking tape.

33.   Blind tacking with metal tacking strip.

KNOTS

Knots have been used for many years—by sailors, for example, for splicing ropes together. There are over forty different types of knots and hitches. In upholstery we need to know but a few of them, for tightening springs, putting on buttons, and so on.

1.   *Overhand knot* is the simplest method of securing the end of cord or twine as well as sewing thread. It is tied at the end to prevent slipping. It is used when you begin sewing to prevent the end from coming through.

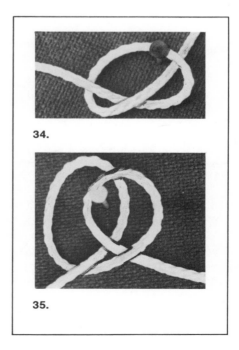

34.

35.

2.   *Clove-hitch knot* is used to fasten the end of spring twine to the nail on the seat frame, for tying the springs together. This knot is simple, strong, and will not slip.

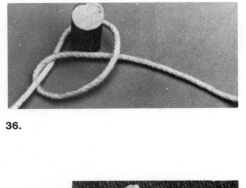

36.

37.

38.

3. *Half-hitch knot* is used to finish the second end of the twine to prevent it from slipping.

4. *Double-hitch knot*. To completely secure the end of the twine, use several half hitches or a double half hitch.

5. *Loop* is used between the coils of the springs. By pulling the loop, it is very easy to position the coil springs.

These are the knots most commonly used in upholstery; a good reference book is the *Boy Scouts of America Handbook*.

STEPS IN REUPHOLSTERING

In most homes you can find an old chair or sofa that needs reupholstering but if you do not have one it is inexpensive to buy one. Once the old piece is in hand, you must then decide how much or how little fixing is needed. The padding might be lumpy or thin. The springs may have come untied and are forcing up from underneath with the webbing sagging. You will be amazed at how quickly your old chair or sofa will shape up into a new handsome piece of furniture.

Just put your chair or sofa upside down on your work bench or sawhorse stand and begin.

Step 1

REMOVING THE CAMBRIC FROM THE BOTTOM

1.   If your chair or sofa has a skirt, remove it.

2.   With a staple remover, pull out all tacks or staples holding the cambric. Remove the cambric, and if it is in good condition save it for reuse.

39.   Stripping the bottom of the chair.

Step 2

REMOVING THE OUTSIDE BACK COVER

1.   Remove all tacks or staples holding the outside back cover at bottom back seat rail.

2.   Remove all tacks or staples holding the outside arm covers at bottom side seat rails in preparation for step 3.

3.   Remove the outside back cover, starting at bottom back seat rail, then the sides and top.

40.   Stripping the outside back of the chair.

41. Stripping the outside arm of the chair.

Step 3

REMOVING THE OUTSIDE ARM COVERS

1. If the arms have front panels, remove them first.

2. Remove all tacks or staples holding the outside arm covers.

3. Remove the outside arm covers completely.

Step 4

OPENING THE INSIDE ARMS AND INSIDE BACK COVERS AT THE SEAT RAILS

This step is necessary both for ease of working and so that measurements for new material can be taken accurately. Place your chair or sofa upright on a work bench or table:

1. Remove all tacks or staples that hold the inside back cover at the back seat rail (a). Tack the bottom of the front back cover (b) to the back tacking strip (c) to secure it in place, to keep the padding in place, and for ease of working.

2. Remove all tacks or staples from both sides of the seat rails that are holding the inside of the arm covers. Tack on the bottom to the arm tacking strip.

Now you can push the tape measure (d) under the back and under the arms for measurement and other work.

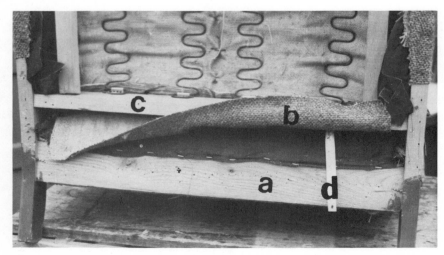

Step 5

REMOVING THE BACK CUSHION

By removing the back outside cover, you can find out about the back cushion. If the cushion is attached to the frame as one separately built cushion, then gently remove the whole back cushion and save it. This will be recovered separately with the new fabric and placed later on the chair or sofa where it belongs.

1. Remove all tacks or staples holding the back cover (b) at the bottom back seat rail (a).

2. Remove all tacks or staples holding the back cover (b) at the back posts (e).

3. See illustration 44. Separate the cushion (g) from the top rail (h) by opening the seam that joins the cushion and the top rail, leaving the padding on. Use a knife or razor.

43.

Step 6

TAKING THE FURNITURE APART

Some chairs or sofas are built so that parts of the frame are assembled by bolting together, for example, recliners, sofa beds, and others. You must take them apart so that you can work on each piece separately. Make sure that you mark each piece for reassembly.

44.

Step 7

FRAME AND WOOD REPAIR

The frame is the foundation of each piece of furniture and will decide the value of the piece of furniture. The frame tells you the style of the furniture. The framework supports all the needed material to complete the piece of furniture. Frames are made of different qualities of wood, and the joints are either glued together or attached in some other way; this also tells you the quality of the piece you are working on.

The proper way of joining or gluing the joints together gives you a strong and dependable frame. If you have or get from someone an old chair or sofa and you decide to reupholster it, check the frame first to see how strong it is and do the repairing before upholstering. For regluing, use clear Liquid Hide Glue; it is easy to work with and makes joints strong.

Shaky joints must be taken apart. If the dowels are shaky pull them out; put glue on the dowels and in the holes. If the dowels are broken, replace with new ones (illustration 45).

45.

All joints must be put together and tightened with furniture clamps. Leave clamped at least for twenty-four hours to dry (see illustration 46).

When wood joints are properly doweled and glued it is not necessary to use hardware for support of shaky frames. Finally, use hardware such as nails, screws, and different angle plates to strengthen joints. Wooden frames sometimes have many large nail holes—fill them up with white carpenter's glue (see illustration 47).

46.   Clamped seat of a chair.

Some furniture is made with finished exposed wood. Refinish, touch up, or revarnish, if needed, before you cover it with final upholstery (see illustration 192).

In case you cannot do repairing or regluing yourself, give the furniture piece to your nearest repair shop.

47. Filling up nail holes with white carpenter's glue.

Step 8

THE SEAT

The seat of a chair or sofa must be built strong enough to hold a person as well as be cushioned for comfort.

Some seats have built-in steel rods at the bottom of the seat for supporting the springs (illustration 48), while others have zigzag springs (illustration 49), metal strips (illustration 50), rubber webbing (illustration 51), or other construction for seat support. Most chairs and sofas have upholstery webbing across the bottom opening to support the springs and make the seat strong enough (illustration 52).

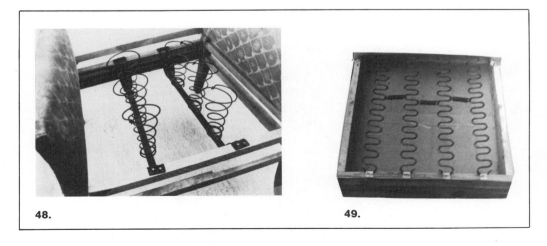

48.   **49.**

51.

50.

52.

I. Applying Steel Webbing

If the webbing has sagged but the springs have not broken through, and the springs are well tied, steel webbing can be applied over the old webbing. Metal webbing should be installed over each row of the springs back to front and side to side as in illustration 53.

53.   **Installed steel webbing.**

Always start from the center first.

1. Nail a steel strip to the outside back seat rail, bend it over the edge, and lay across the frame over the center row of springs (see illustration 54).

54. Installing steel webbing.

55. Tightening the steel webbing with a stretching tool.

2. Place the webbing tool as in illustration 55, then pull the steel strip taut and nail it in with a twine nail to the bottom of the frame.

3. Cut off the steel strip, leaving a 2″ to 3″ end, bend over the edge and nail it in with a # 12 or # 14 tack to the side of the frame (see illustration 54).

Note: By nailing the end of the steel strip to the side of the frame (bending it over the edge), it makes a strong support.

4. Do the same to all the rows of the springs going from back to front, then from side to side, weaving it under and over the metal strips. After finishing, it should look like illustration 53.

II. Rewebbing

If the webbing has been broken, new webbing should be installed. Always attach the center webbing piece first, since this applies pressure to the frame and tightens it. Decide how many strips of webbing you will need each way, noting that no more than 1″ should separate them. You will need some #12 and #6 tacks to fasten the webbing, a webbing stretcher, and a hammer to complete the job.

Use the following procedure:

1. Place the frame upside down on a workbench or table.

2. Fold the end of the webbing over about 1 1/2″, with the folded end on top. Tack with five #12 staggered tacks to the bottom of the seat frame at the back.

3. Pull the webbing across the frame toward you. Place the webbing stretcher under the overhanging webbing 2 1/2″ from the frame. Insert the teeth into the webbing from underneath as in illustration 56. Pull the webbing taut and tack with five #6 tacks, release the stretcher, cut off the remaining webbing 1 1/2″ past the edge of the frame, and fold over on top. Tack with five #12 staggered tacks. Fasten all the back-to-front strips similarly.

4. Tack down all side-to-side strips similarly, weaving each crosswise strip under and over the lengthwise ones, as in illustration 57.

5. Turn your project right side up.

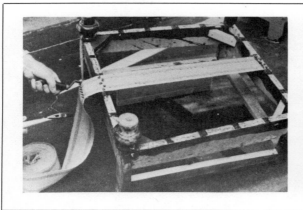

56. **Using a webbing stretcher to pull the webbing tightly.**

57. **Installed webbing.**

III. Installing Coil Springs

After you have installed the webbing, the next step is to install the coil springs. It is important to know that coil springs have a top and bottom. On top, the spring wire is either bent down (1) or twisted around the first coil (2) to prevent it from wearing the padding (see illustration 58). They should be evenly spaced in as straight rows as possible to simplify tying. With a little care you can arrange them in a neat pattern and form a good foundation for a strong seat.

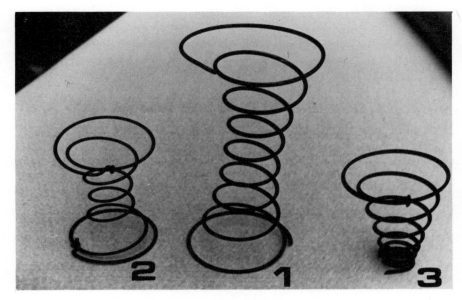

58. Coil springs.

1. On top, the spring wire is bent down.

2. On top, the spring wire is twisted around the first coil.

3. Spring for metal bar.

On the flat seat, place the front springs close to the front of the seat rail. For rounded seat, the springs are laid back from the frame, from 1/2″ to 3″, depending on how many springs are installed inside the frame.

The following steps should be taken:

1. Set the springs temporarily on the webbing, evenly spaced.

2. Mark with chalk the position of each spring on the webbing.

3. Remove all but one, which you will begin sewing.

4. Space four stitches per spring evenly around the bottom coil, using a 6″ or 8″ long straight needle, stitching through the webbing close to the spring coil and back down the other side of it. Tie the first stitch.

5. Take the next stitch about a quarter of the way around the coil, and so on. Repeat sewing each spring to the webbing with four stitches (see illustration 59).

Note: Start sewing the back row of the springs to the webbing first. Do not make knots at each stitch position. Make knots at the beginning and at the end of the sewing twine only.

59. **Stitch pattern (bottom of chair). The dark circles indicate the springs position; white squares indicate the sewing twine; white dots indicate the stitches over the coil springs.**

IV. Tying the Springs

Properly tying the springs gives shape, comfort, durability, and good looks to a seat surface. Springs are tied back to front, side to side, diagonally, and between the rows of the springs. Therefore, each spring will be tied a total of eight times when you are finished. The tying process should begin at the center of the middle row of springs. Back to front ties are made first to keep the springs from moving backward or forward. Next tie the springs side to side, making sure all springs stand perfectly upright when the twine is secured. The diagonal rows are then tied, and finally twine-to-twine ties are made between rows to give a finished netlike look. It is important that the springs are not more than 2″ over the seat railing upon completion.

1. Set twine nails halfway in on the tops of the seat rails at the center of each row of springs, diagonal rows, and between rows (see illustration 60).

60.

2. Cut pieces of spring twine for all the ties, making them about double length for flat seats and 1 3/4 times for rounded seats.

3. With a clove-hitch knot, secure one end of the twine to the nails on the back seat rail, leaving 8″ twine for a return tie for a flat seat, and drive the nails in for permanent bond (see illustration 61).

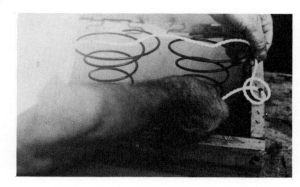

61.

4. If you have a flat seat, that is, a seat that has a loose cushion, feed the twine from the back seat rail (1) to the third rung of the nearest spring (2) in the middle row, and make an overhand knot (3). Then feed the twine to the top rung (4) of the same spring, toward you (see illustration 62).

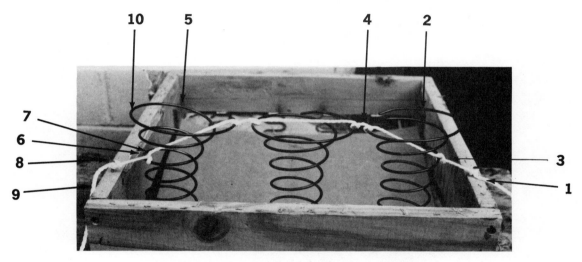

62.   Springs tied for a flat seat in the middle row.

If you have a rounded seat, that is, a seat without a loose cushion, your first tie from the nail (1) will be to the top rung (2) of the nearest spring (3) in the middle row (see illustration 63).

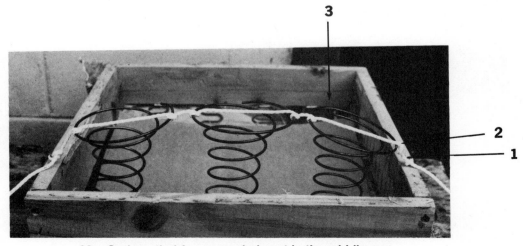

63.   Springs tied for a rounded seat in the middle row.

5.   Connect all springs of a row by looping the twine around opposite sides of each top coil, except for a flat seat, where the last spring (5), outer side, is tied with an overhand knot (6) on the third rung (7), before being tied to the nail (8) with a double overhand knot, and the nail driven in. For a flat seat, leave an excess of twine (9) at the beginning and on the end so that you can return the twine from the nail (8) and tie to the top coil of the spring (10).

6.   Repeat similarly, tying all rows back to front, side to side, diagonally, and between rows.

7.   Return all loose ends (1), and tie, on a flat seat, to the outer edge (2) of the springs (see illustration 64). Make sure that the edges are flat with the rest of the seat.

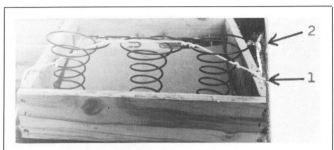

64.

Steps in Tying the Springs

1.   With a clove-hitch knot, tie the spring twine to the nail on the seat rail.

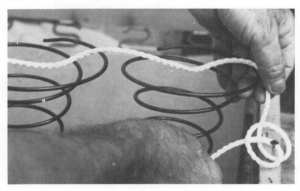

65.

2.   Make an overhand knot on the top rung of the nearest spring for a rounded seat and on the third rung for a flat seat. Thread the twine under the opposite side of the coil.

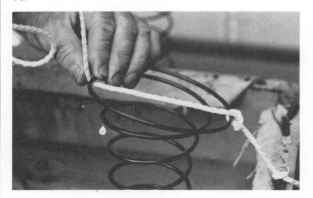

66.

3. Bring the twine back over the coil and under the twine and pull it away from you.

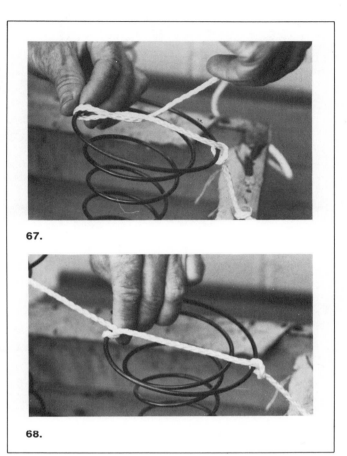

67.

4. Pull the twine toward you to complete your lock loop.

68.

Note: This is the method used for tying all the springs.

Your completed project should look like illustration 69 for a flat seat and illustration 70 for a rounded seat.

69.   Springs tied for a flat seat.

70. **Springs tied for a rounded seat.**

71. **Springs tied for a small seat.**

On small seats of a chair, it is not necessary to tie the springs diagonally. It is good enough to tie them back to front, side to side, and between the rows of the springs (see illustration 71).

V. Covering the Springs

On all open framed pieces of furniture, whether it be coil springs, webbing, zigzag springs, or other means that support the seat, this must be covered with burlap or other heavy material to keep a loose stuffing from going through or between the springs or webbing. It also provides a smoother foundation for the padding.

1. Cut a piece of burlap 3″ wider and 3″ longer than the area to be covered.

2. Start at the middle front of a seat railing, overturn the burlap twice at the end, and tack with #4 or #6 tacks, depending on wood hardness. Tack about the middle third of the front edge, spacing tacks 1″ apart.

3. Tighten straight toward the opposite edge, overturn the burlap twice, and tack as above. Repeat on the other two sides.

4. Continue tacking from the midpoints to the corners, finishing the burlaping over the springs (see illustration 72).

Note: On a weak frame you may tack the burlap on the sides of the seat frame (see illustration 73).

72. Cover springs with burlap, turn ends twice to the top, and tack.

burlap

73.

VI. Installing Edge Roll

The edge roll is needed both for comfort and appearance. If the original is in good condition, it can be reused. Its purpose is to shape the edge of the frame of the chair and keep the stuffing from working away from the edges, thus keeping the edges from wearing the upholstery material (see illustration 74).

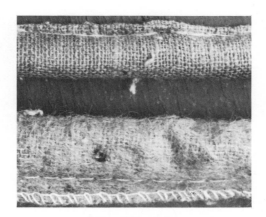

74. Edge rolls.

On some wooden edged frames with open sides and back, we tack edge roll to all four sides (see illustration 75). With just open sides and a closed back, edge rolls are used on three sides (see illustration 76). On closed sides and back, just the front is done (see illustration 77).

75.

76.

77.

Corners must be mitered, and the edging should be installed flush with the sides of the frame, nailed firmly to the wood.

On the spring edges, edge roll is used to cushion the hardness of the wire. It is installed as for wooden frames, except it is sewn to the exposed spring edges to provide comfort and protection, using 1″-wide stitches. Sewn properly to the springs, it will cut down wear caused by friction on the cloth (see illustration 78).

78.   The edge roll is sewn to the spring edge.

Proceed sewing edge roll to the spring edge:

1.   Take a large curved needle with a long piece of sewing twine.
2.   Secure the end of the twine at the place you want to start.
3.   Push the needle through the burlap under the spring edge (see illustration 79).
4.   Grab the twine and put the needle through the loop and pull tight (see illustration 80).
5.   Continue similarly until you have finished.
     This method of sewing the edge roll secures it firmly to the spring edge.

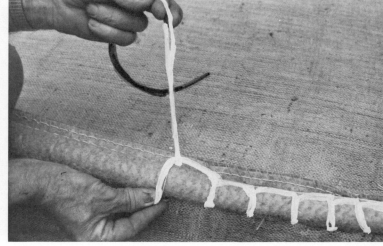

79.   80.

VII. Padding

Padding gives shape and softness to upholstery; how well you do your job with padding will affect the looks and life of the upholstery. There are many different methods of padding:

1. Cotton: Tear or pull the cotton apart, then fill in the depressed areas and corners firmly with cotton (see illustration 81). On top place a layer of cotton long enough to push underneath the arms and back of the chair or sofa. Use enough so that you cannot feel the springs through the padding, which will be about 1″ thick for a seat with a loose cushion or flat seat. Next smooth the padding out in all directions. Padding with moss or hair is done in the same way.

For smoothness, comfort, and a good appearance, put a 1/2″ layer of polyfoam over the cotton (see illustration 82), again long enough to push under the arms and back of your project.

For a rounded seat, the amount of padding used depends upon how high your seat will be; usually up to 4″ to 6″ of padding is used. Again you may use a thin layer of polyfoam.

81. Fill in the depressed areas and corners firmly with cotton.

82. For smoothness, comfort, and good appearance, put a ½″ layer of polyfoam over the cotton.

2. Foam rubber: This is a spongy mass that is easy to handle and has many uses in upholstery for padding seats, arms, backs, and cushions. It is graded in soft, medium, and hard and comes in different thicknesses. It can be cemented together or to another material with rubber cement by coating both surfaces with cement, allowing to dry until tacky, and then pressing together. The resulting joint will be stronger than the surrounding foam.

To cut foam rubber up to 2″ thick, use shears. For thicker pieces, cut with a handsaw. To do this properly, you should first mark a cutting line, then place under the foam a 3″-wide board so that the cutting line falls somewhere over the board with the ends of the foam overhanging. Now with a saw slowly cut vertically through the foam (see illustration 83).

For cutting a round form use a narrow handsaw (see illustration 84).

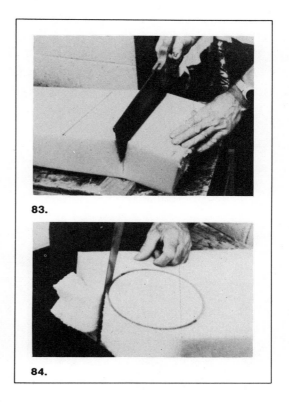

83.

84.

　　　　To pad a flat seat, use 1″-thick foam rubber, which is also good for webbed seats, while 2″-thick should be used for coil and zigzag springs, which are covered with burlap. For a rounded seat, the thickness is determined by how high your seat will be as with cotton padding above. Always add 1/2″ to the exact dimensions to cover the hard edges.
　　　　Foam rubber gives you comfort and saves you upholstery time in comparison to other types of padding.

VIII.　Covering with Muslin

　　　　A muslin cover holds the stuffing or padding to a planned shape and provides a smooth even surface for installing the top cover. It is used on all seats, inside arms, backs, and wings. The muslin should be pulled very tight and tacked as near the padding as possible. When tacking muslin on a rounded seat, tack it temporarily on one side, pull it tightly to the opposite side, and tack it permanently. The padding will be moved slightly to the pulling side. Now go back and remove the tacks on the temporarily tacked side and pull tightly, while bringing the padding back to its original position, and tack permanently. Repeat on all sides, marking and cutting slips for posts on arms or backs.

Generally:

1.　Cut a piece of muslin for covering the needed area, leaving about a 2″ excess on each side for ease of handling.

2.   Lay the muslin over the padding, tack it in place to the frame. Always start in the middle of the railing and work to the corners, spacing tacks 1″ apart.

3.   Make several small pleats on rounded corners and curves (see illustration 85). Make a single butterfly pleat for square corners (see illustration 86).

If the padded surface is not firm, fill it in with cotton padding. Remember the muslin will give the final shape to your furniture.

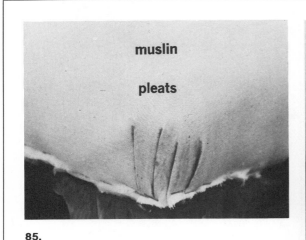

85.

86.

IX.   Tufting the Seat Down

On seats without loose cushions—rounded seats—you must tuft the seat down. When the padding is completed and covered with muslin and not more than 1″ thick, you are ready for the final covering, but if it is more than 1″ thick you must tuft (stitch) the seat down no matter what type of padding you have used. This is a temporary process, because after tufting the seat down, the final covering is applied and then the tufting twine is cut on the bottom of the seat and the seat will puff out giving a smooth, tight covering. If this is not done, the seat covering will be loose, and get looser with wear.

The materials you will need are a straight 12″ or 14″ long needle and sewing twine (do not double). For cotton padding it is better to use a 3 square point needle. Also identify your sewing twine so that, when finished, you will cut the tufting twine and not the spring twine.

1.   Thread about 3 yards of sewing twine into an upholsterer's needle.

2.   Secure one end of the twine in the center on the bottom of the seat.

3. Make 2″ or 3″ spaced stitches through the webbing, springs, and stuffing, following a pattern similar to the form of your seat (see illustrations 87 and 88).

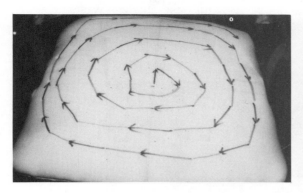

87.

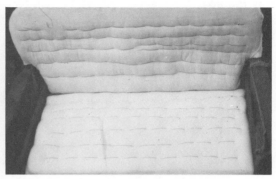

88.

4. Now go back and with one hand press down the seat at the first stitch. Pull tight the twine with your other hand and hold so that it will not go back (see illustration 89). Continue pressing and pulling until you come to the last stitch, then secure the end as you did the beginning of the twine.

5. Continue as above, using a new piece of twine as necessary, until you are finished.

When the seat has been tufted down snugly, you are ready to apply your final cover. After your final cover has been put on, cut all stitches of the tufting twine from under the seat.

89.

X. The Final Cover

Since the final cover is visible, it is important to do an especially good job of putting it on. If your chair or sofa has good padding on the arm and back, you may begin putting on the final cover after getting the seat ready. If repadding is needed, do it first before putting the final cover on the seat. Next, you must make a final decision as to which direction the weave lines will run, not only on your seat but on the whole project. It is recommended that if your upholstery fabric pattern permits you to cut it in the railroaded way (parallel to the selvage edges), it should be cut this way for ease and less waste. You will have fewer seams, since long pieces can be cut in one piece. Make sure you center the pattern (see illustrations 90 and 91).

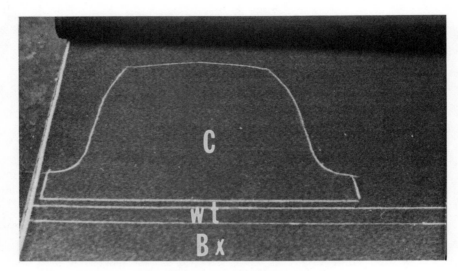

90.   Normal 54″ width marked.

91.   Railroaded marked.

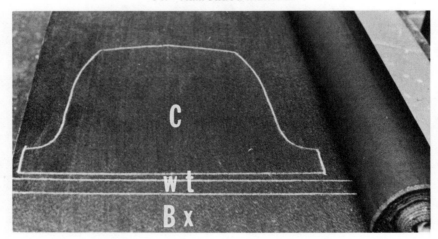

Seats of chairs and sofas vary in their construction, shape, and feel. Thus, many seats will require their own particular work. To simplify matters so that you can understand the main principle of how to install the final seat cover, I will classify the seats into two main groups:

1. *Flat seats* are those seats that have a loose cushion, some with T-form-style seats, others non-T-form style.

2. *Rounded seats* are those without a loose cushion, and also vary in their forms.

COVERING THE T-FORM SEAT

We will recover a piped-back wing chair.

The seat cover consists of two pieces: the top seat cover (1) and the band (front seat) (2) (see illustration 92).

Follow these steps:

92.   Piped-back wing chair.

1. Make a plan paper (code ''S'' for seat and ''Bd'' for band).

2. Measure the seat, from the band on top (a) to the back seat railing, pushing the tape measure under the back (b) (see illustration 94). Add 3″ total allowance for seam joining with the band and for tacking to the back seat rail. Write the dimension on the paper plan. For the chair in illustration 92 it is 26″.

3. Measure side to side, widest points only, between side seat railings, pushing the tape measure under the arms (c) and (d) (see illustration 94), and again add 3″ allowance. This dimension for the chair in illustration 92 is 30″.

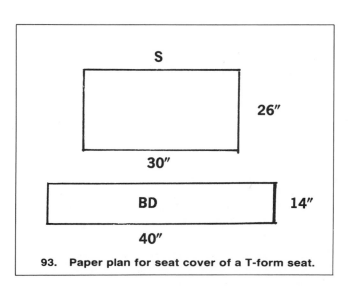

93.   Paper plan for seat cover of a T-form seat.

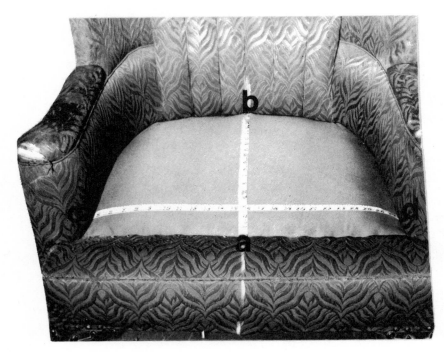

94.

4.   See illustration 95. Measure the band from the front of the top seat (e) to the bottom of the front seat railing (f), add 3″ allowance for the seam joining the top seat panel (e) and for tacking to the bottom seat railing (f). Write the dimension on the paper plan; here it is 14″ with allowance.

5.   Measure side to side, front of the seat, as in illustration 95, from the left arm post (g) to the right arm post (h). Add 3″ allowance for tacking. Write the dimension on the paper plan; here it is 40″ with allowance.

6.   On the finishing (right) side of your fabric, mark the cutting lines in chalk as per the dimensions on your paper plan. Mark also the midpoints of the front and back edges of the seat, and top and bottom of the band. Cut out the pieces in rectangular forms.

7.   On the reverse side, mark in code the names of each piece (S—seat, Bd—band) and indicate with arrows the direction that the panels will lie. For velvet material, the nap on the top of the seat must be from the back to the front. It should feel smooth from back to front. On the band the nap should go from the bottom to the top, and also feel smooth in this direction.

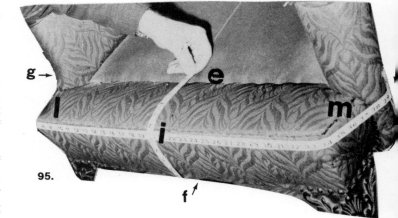

95.

8.   Preparations to finish the band:
  a) Place the band inside out on the table.
  b) Measure your chair seat from seam (e) to the front top edge (i) (see illustration 95), and add 1″ allowance for seam (e). On the chair in illustration 92 this is 5″ with the allowance. Transfer this dimension to your band and draw a chalk-mark line (k) along the band as in illustration 96.

c) Measure from the side top edge (l) to the other side top edge (m) (see illustration 95). On the chair in illustration 92, it is exactly 30″. Transfer this dimension to your band, making sure the midpoint mark is in the center. Mark lines (n) perpendicular to line (k) on each end; these are sewing lines. On each end of the band we have square corners (o) (see illustration 96). Mark cutting lines (p), 1″ inside the corners from sewing lines (n) and (k), and cut out (o).

96.

9.   Fold one of the corners (o) inside out so that the sewing lines (k) and (n) line up (see illustration 97). Sew the corner by machine, starting from the corner (r) and along the marked sew line to the end (s) in the direction of the arrow. The fabric will stretch from the corner (r) to the end (s) (see illustration 98). Go back, as in illustration 99, and sew a slight curve to the inside of the corner. Repeat for the other corner. When you finish sewing the corner, turn the corner right side up. It will look like the finished corner in illustration 100.

97.   Folding corner for sewing.

98.   Folded corner for sewing.

99.   For final sewing of the corner, follow the arrow.

100.   Finished corner.

10.   Turn the band right side up and recheck for fit. If the corners do not fit right, sew the puffy places until the band fits perfectly.

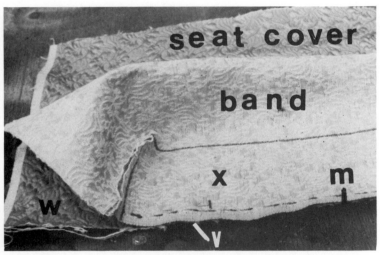
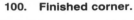

101.   Seat cover and band sewed together inside out.

11.   See illustration 101. Lay the top of the band (x) together with the front of the seat cover (w), and finish sides so that the midpoint marks (m) are together. Sew together by machine, making the seam about 1/2″ from ends (v). The sewing is done on the "wrong side" of the fabric.

12.   See illustration 102. Lay the band (r) on the front seat so that the band panel is in position right side up. Draw the top seat panel (s) to the front, exposing the joining seam (t) on the wrong side of the fabric. Using an 8″ straight long needle and sewing twine, sew through the exposed seam (t) to the chair seat, making about 3/4″ stitches. If the previous final cover has been left on, and its seam is good, use a 3″ or 4″ curved needle and sew to this seam. Secure the twine end.

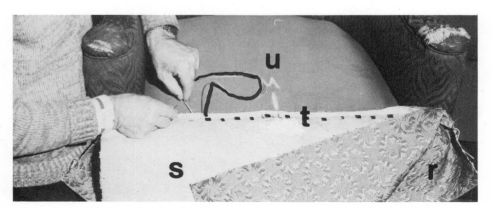

102.

13. Mark, with chalk, the midpoints of the back seat railing outside the back and the bottom front seat railing. Draw the top seat panel (s) to the back. Lay the seat panel (s) over the seat (u) so that the top of the seat panel (s) is in position to cover the seat (u).

14. See illustration 103. Slip the seat cover under the arms (v) and under the back (w) of the chair so that panel midpoint marks (x) line up with railing midpoint mark. Stretch the cover tightly and evenly in all directions, make cuts for posts, and tack to the seat railing on all sides.

The tacked seat cover should look as it does in illustration 103.

Note: For saving upholstery fabric, you can use stretchers under the arms and back of your chair or sofa (see illustration 104). These inexpensive pieces of strong material are double-stitched to the final cover and extend it for pulling and tacking in place where it is not seen.

103. Seat installed.

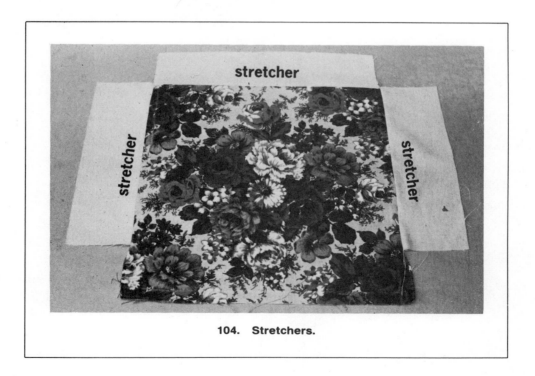

104. Stretchers.

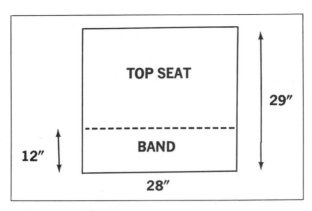

105. Paper plan for non-T-form seat.

COVERING THE NON-T-FORM SEAT

1. Make a paper plan for the seat covering in rectangular form for the top seat and band (see illustration 105).

2. See illustration 106. Measure the seat from the bottom of the front seat railing (1) to the back seat railing, pushing the tape measure under the back (2); add 4″ total allowance for handling. Put the total dimension on the paper plan (example, 29″).

106. Taking measurements for the seat.

3. Measure the band from the seam (3) on the top of the seat to the bottom of the front seat railing (1); add 1″ allowance for the seam (3), and add 1 1/2″ for tacking to the bottom of the seat railing (1). Put the dimension on the paper plan (example, 12″).

4. Measure, side to side, between side railings, widest point only; add 3″ allowance for tacking and put the dimension on the paper plan (example, 28″).

5. On the finishing side of the fabric, mark the cutting lines in chalk as per dimensions (28″ x 29″), and cut out.

6. On the reverse side, mark in code the name of this piece (S—seat), an arrow indicating the direction the panel will lie on the seat, and a chalk line for the seam (12″ from bottom to top) as in illustration 107.

107. Reverse side of the seat cover.

7. Sew the seam about 1/2″ with a sewing machine (see illustration 108).

108. Fold seat cover on the chalk line and sew the seam.

109. Velvet covers (arrows show the direction of the nap).

The seat cover must be made from two pieces when covering with velvet. (See the explanation below.) On the left side of illustration 109, two pieces of velvet are sewn together so that in the top piece (S) (horizontal position) the direction of the nap is from the back to the front. In the front piece of velvet (B), the direction of the nap is from the bottom to the top. The top of the seat cover (S) and the band cover (B) have the same color.

On the right side of illustration 109, the top piece (S1) and the band cover (B1) are one solid piece of velvet, and the top piece is a lighter color than the front band cover due to the direction of the nap. This is the reason that the seat cover (top seat and band) must be made from two pieces of material and sewn together.

8. See illustration 110. Lay the seat cover (6) over the seat so that the top of the seat cover (6) is in position to cover the top seat. Draw the band (7) to the back, exposing the seam (8) that joins the top seat (6) and band (7) together on the wrong side. Arrange the seam about 3″ to the back from the front top edge (9), slip under the arms (a), stretch the seam tight, and temporarily tack the seam to the frame on both sides, and sew to the seat.

Note: Watch that midpoint marks (m) join.

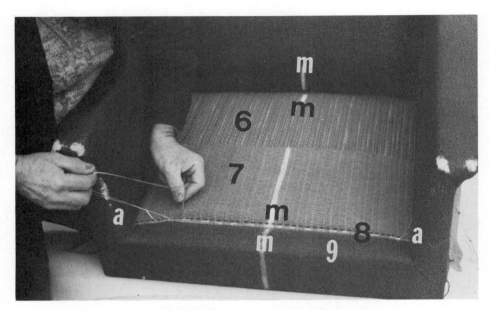

110.   Sewing final seat cover to the seat.

9.   See illustrations 111–115. Draw the band to the front and tack under the bottom of the front seat rail so that the midpoint mark on the band and the midpoint mark on the frame join. Stretch the top cover tight and evenly in all directions, and make cuts for back and arm posts. Then tack to the seat railing on all sides.

111.   Completely tacked final seat cover.

Steps in covering the seat:

1.   Sew the final cover to the seat as in illustration 110.
2.   Draw the band to the front as in illustration 112.

3. Fold the sides of the cover to the top, and cut openings for the arm posts as in illustrations 113 and 114.

4. Fold the back side of the cover to the front and cut for the back posts as in illustration 115.

5. Tack the seat cover to the frame on all sides as in illustration 111.

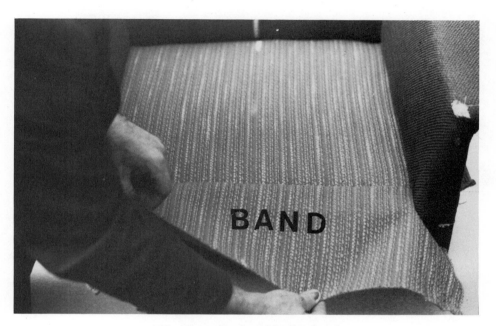

112.   Draw the band to the front.

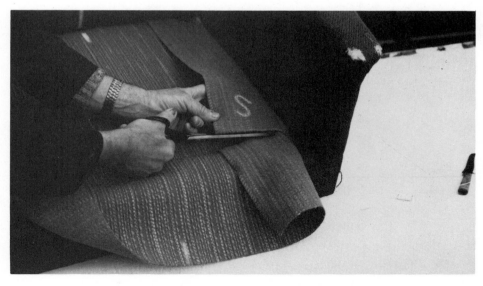

113.   Fold sides (s) and cut an opening for arm posts.

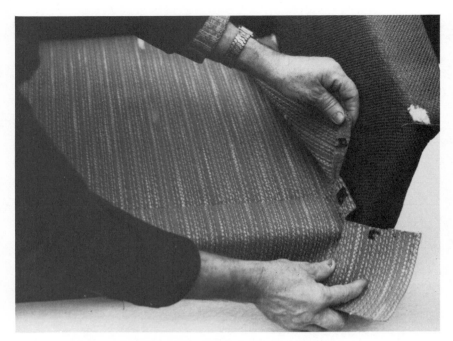

114. Cut an opening for the arm post.

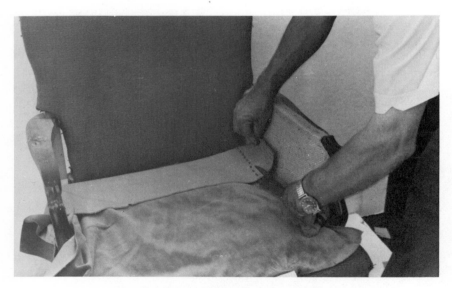

115. Fold the back side of the seat cover and cut openings for the back posts.

COVERING A SEAT THAT HAS EXPOSED BACK AND ARM POSTS

As we look at the chair in illustration 116, with exposed back and arm posts, it looks very simple to cover the seat but this is not so, especially if you wish to use vinyl or leather. Any slight mistake in cutting the fabric for fitting around the back and arm posts will spoil your seat-cover piece. To cover the seat of a chair with exposed back and arm posts, you need the exact dimensions and the fabric must be cut exactly. Follow these directions:

back post

arm post

116.   Chair with exposed back and arm posts.

1.   See illustration 117. Take a measurement from the bottom seat rail side (a) to the side (b), add 3″ for handling. For example, if it is 25″, with allowance, it is 28″.

2.   Take a measurement from the bottom front seat railing (c) to the bottom back seat railing (d), add 3″ for handling. For example, if it is 24″, with allowance, it is 27″.

Note: All measurements are taken at the widest points only, side to side, or front to back.

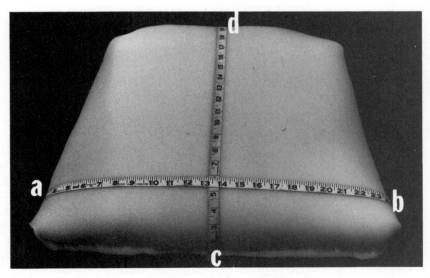

117.   Measurements of the seat.

3. Cut from your upholstery fabric a rectangular form 27″ from front to back and 28″ from side to side (27″ x 28″), for example.

4. Lay the seat cover on the table, inside out.

5. See illustration 118. Make a center line (c) from the front to the back.

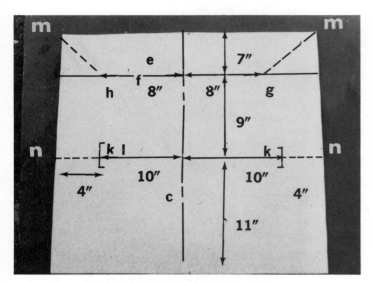

118. Diagram for cutting seat cover.

6. Take a measurement from the bottom of the back seat railing to the top of the back seat railing with padding at the posts (g and h in illustration 116). Add 1 1/2″ allowance for tacking to the bottom of the back seat railing. In this example it is 7″, with allowance, as in illustration 118, dimension (e).

7. Make a line (f) from one side to the other side.

8. Take a measurement between the back posts (g and h in illustration 116). In this example it is 16″ between the back posts. This is 8″ from the center line, c, to each back post.

9. Take a measurement from back posts (g and h) to the arm posts (i) in illustration 116. In this example it is 9″, line f to line l, in illustration 118.

10. Make a line (l) from one side to the other side. It passes through the center of the arm posts (see illustration 118).

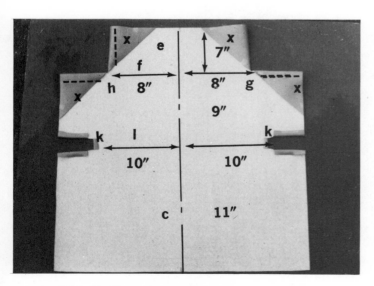

119. Cutting the seat cover for fitting around back and arm posts.

11. From the back corners (m), make a cut to the back-post marks (g) and (h), and from the edges (n) cut along line (l) to the arm-post marks (k) as in illustration 118.

12. Put the seat cover in position on the seat of the chair so that the midpoint mark in the back and in the front of the seat cover and the seat frame line up. Cut out excess (x), leaving about 2″ for folding underneath for fitting around the posts (see illustration 119). The excess for the arm posts (k) is already cut out and the excess (x) for the back posts is marked for cutting. To avoid a mistake in cutting, do not cut too close to the points (g, h, and k), for fitting, then cut more if necessary.

13. Tack the seat cover all around to the bottom of the seat railings. For decorative finishing, use upholstery decorative nails as in illustration 116.

Note: Fit the cover around the back, arm posts, and legs as in illustrations 120 and 121.

120. Fitting to the three sides of post.

121. Fitting to two sides of post.

Alternate Method of Fitting the Seat Cover

1. Cut a piece of upholstery fabric to cover the entire seat.

2. Put the cover on the seat in position, and temporarily tack the front and back of the seat cover, midpoint marks only.

3. First fit the seat cover around the arm posts by folding and cutting it as in illustration 122. Tack both sides of the seat cover to the side railings.

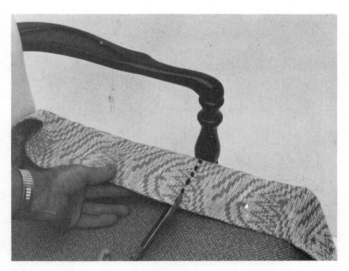

122. Cutting arm-post opening.
123. Cutting back-post opening.

4. Untack the back side of the seat cover and fit around the back posts by folding and cutting it as in illustration 123.

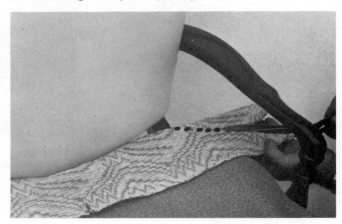

5. Tack the seat cover all around to the seat frame, except the front seat rail, which is tacked up to 4″ from the front corners (see illustration 124).

6. Now to complete the front corners, tack side (s) completely from the back to the front corner (c), then pull the pleat (f) over the corner (c), and tack as in illustration 125. Complete the other corner the same way.

124. Tacked front edge.

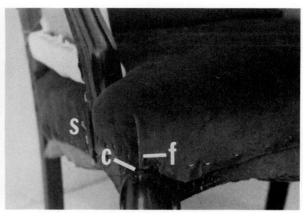

125. Completed corner.

COVERING THE SEAT THAT HAS EXPOSED WOOD

Some chairs and sofas have exposed finished wood all around the seat, some on three sides and others in the front only. Some have exposed wood on arms and on the back too. (See the chairs with exposed wood in illustrations 126–133.)

The seat cover may consist of one piece, the seat cover (a), as in illustration 126, or a seat cover (b), with a border (c), as in illustration 127.

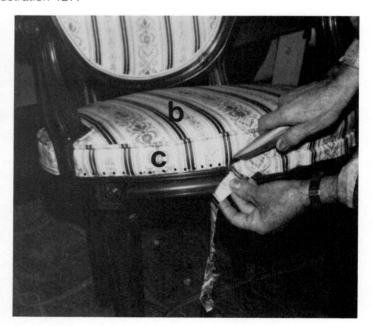

127. Trimming excess material from the seat edge.

126. One-piece seat.

1. Staple or tack the seat cover close to the wood edge, then trim with a razor blade or trimming knife as in illustration 127.

2. Finish the edge of the seat cover, conceal the staples and tacks, and achieve a decorative finish by applying gimp on old-fashioned projects and double cording on modern pieces.

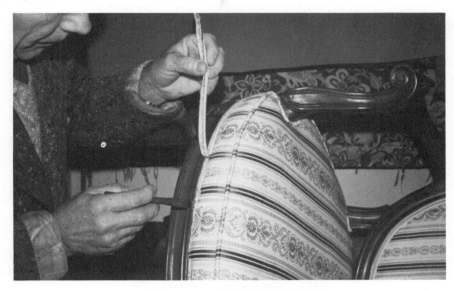

128.   Installing double cording.

INSTALLING DOUBLE CORDING

Double cording is used for the same purpose as gimp, the only difference being that double cording is used on modern furniture and should be installed without upholstery decorative nails. Double cording should be glued into place with a special glue for fabrics. Apply glue on the wrong side of the double cording and on the place where the double cording will be installed. Then press the double cording into place with your fingers. On curved edges, fasten with tacks about a quarter way in for the time being as in illustration 129. After about an hour pull the tacks out and the job will be done (see illustration 130).

129.   Installing double cording to the curved edge.

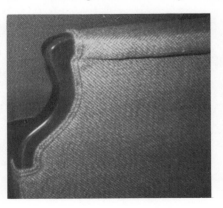

130.

INSTALLING GIMP

Gimp is a long band of fancy braiding in 1/2″ width that comes in many styles and rich colors. It is used for covering the tacks and staples along the edges of upholstered pieces and adds a decorative look for old-fashioned furniture. Gimp can be installed with upholstery decorative nails as in illustration 126 or with fabric glue as in illustration 131.

131.   Gimp is installed with glue.

Gluing gimp in place is a simple but slow process. Apply glue to the gimp, on the wrong side, and to the place where the gimp will be glued. Apply the glue to 6″ to 8″ of gimp and press in place, then glue another 6″ to 8″ of gimp. Repeat this procedure until all the gimp is glued. Use a wet cloth to wipe off any excess glue.

NAIL TRIM

On many modern and provincial pieces the trim is a basic part of the overall design. Nail trim is used for holding the edges of the upholstery in place and for decorative design as in illustration 132, or just for overall decorative finish as in illustration 133.

132.   Nail trim is used for holding the edges and for decorative design.

The spacing of upholstery decorative nails is a matter of personal taste. You can place the nailheads in a solid line or space them. To make sure the spacing is even, first determine the desired distance between the heads of the nails, then take a piece of hard paper of this width and use as a guide for spacing between the nails.

133.   Nail trim is used for decorative design.

SUMMARY OF STEPS IN FINISHING THE SEAT

134.   Repair the frame of the project.

135.   Install base support of the seat (webbing, steel bars, or other support), then install and tie the springs.

136.   Cover the springs with burlap.

137.   Install edge roll.

138.   Fill in the depressed areas and corners firmly with cotton.

139.   Cover with as many layers of cotton as you need.

140.   Cover the cotton with muslin.

141.   Tuft the seat down for rounded seat.

142.   Install the final cover.

OTHER SEATS (REPAIRING AND COVERING)

I. Flat Padded Seats

Flat padded seats are built on wood as in illustration 143 or on an open frame as in illustration 144. Flat padded seats are used on dining-room chairs, desk chairs, and stool seats. If the support on the open frame (see illustration 144) of the seat has been worn out, replace it with webbing as in illustration 146 or with 3/8″ thick plywood as in illustration 147. Then put a light padding on top of the webbing or plywood (use cotton, foam, or other fillings) and put on the final seat cover.

143.

144.

145. Chairs with padded seats.

1. Measure the seat side to side, back to front, widest points only.

2. Cut a seat cover, with 1 1/2″ allowance on each side.

3. Place the cover on the seat and tack it to the bottom of all sides of the seat, starting in the center of each side and going to the corners.

4. On the bottom of the seat, on the corners, make butterfly folds, cut the excess material, and tack (see illustration 148).

5. For neatness, the bottom of the seat can be covered with cambric or hard paper.

146. Open-seat frame repaired with webbing.

147. Open-seat frame repaired with plywood.

148. Cutting the excess of material.

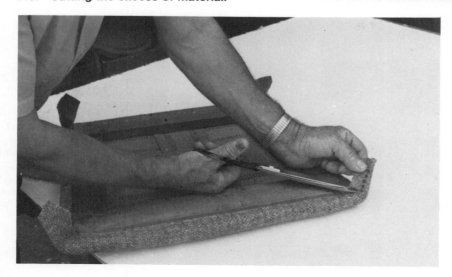

II. Rounded Seats

All seats with loose cushions are flat seats (illustration 150,) are constructed in different ways, and are not heavily padded. All seats without loose cushions are rounded seats (illustrations 149, 151, and 152), which are constructed differently and are heavily padded. Some could be constructed with coil springs supported by webbing or steel bars, but now most seats are constructed with zigzag springs. We have already learned how to repair a seat with coil springs. Now we will learn how to repair seats with zigzag springs. If you are recovering a seat with zigzag springs, chances are good that you will have to do some repair work on the springs. Most zigzag springs are constructed poorly. They often are not nailed to the frame properly or are not spaced closely enough so that the padding (cotton, foam, or other fibers) goes through the springs and gives a lumpy seat. By running your hand over the top of your seat you can feel if your seat support is well constructed.

149. Rounded seat without a border.

150. Flat seat.

151. Rounded seat with open arms and open back.

152.   Rounded seat with border.

If your seat is lumpy, you will have to repair it. If you are going to repair your seat constructed with zigzag springs, you should refine your seat by tying your springs with spring twine as in illustration 153.

Tie the springs to the seat rails in the directions as in illustration 153 to avoid pulling the springs to one side, and between the rows. Tie the spring twine, using an overhand knot, to the bands of the springs.

Upon finishing, you will have a netlike seat with small openings so that your padding will not go through the zigzag springs and your seat will be smooth for a long time.

Note: On a heavy frame, use spring twine nails; on a weak frame, use # 14 tacks to avoid splitting the wood.

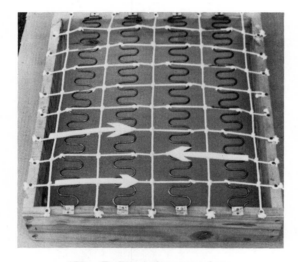

153.   Refined zigzag springs.

The final covering:

The rounded seat cover may consist of one piece (a) as in illustration 149, or two pieces, (a) the top of the seat cover with (o) the border, as in illustration 152.

Measure widest points. Allow 3″ total for handling.

1.   For furniture with open arms, measure from the bottom seat rail on one side to the bottom seat rail on the other side. This is because the seat cover must hide the seat rail as in illustration 151. For furniture with closed arms (see illustration 152), measure from the top seat rail on one side to the top seat rail on the other side.

2.   Measure from the bottom of the front seat rail to the bottom of the back seat rail, for an open back seat. For a closed back seat, measure to the top of the back seat rail.

3.   Take measurements for the border, if you wish to install one.

4.   Cut, in rectangular form, upholstery fabric according to the measurements.

5. Mark midpoint marks in the front and the back on the seat frame and also on the seat covers.

6. Lay the seat cover on the chair or sofa seat so the midpoint marks line up, and tack to the seat frame, starting in the middle of each side and then going to the corners. Tack to the bottom of the seat railing all around for furniture with open arms and back. On closed arms, tack to the top side rails (outside). On a closed back, tack to the top of the back rail (outside). The front of the seat cover is tacked to the bottom of the front seat rail. Install a border if you wish.

III. Loose Cushion Seats with Metal Straps and Coil Springs

Platform chairs have a seat built for comfort cushioning. The seat and back cushions are made separately and they are loose.

Metal straps and coil tension springs are used for seat support. Metal straps with coil tension springs are attached to the frame with heavy screw eyes as in illustration 155. If you have broken straps, springs, or screw eyes, replace them with good ones. You can find metal straps and coil tension springs in old bedsprings. Or buy them in a hardware store or upholstery shop. Metal straps can be made from metal webbing by cutting it into pieces of the desired length that you need.

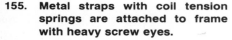

154. Loose cushion seat with metal straps.

155. Metal straps with coil tension springs are attached to frame with heavy screw eyes.

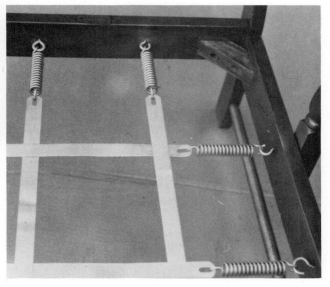

IV.   Loose Cushion Seats with Rubber Webbing

This is the same as the seat with metal straps, except instead of metal straps use rubber webbing. This seat is more cushioned than others. Clips that fit into slots in the seat rails are mounted on the ends of the rubber strips.

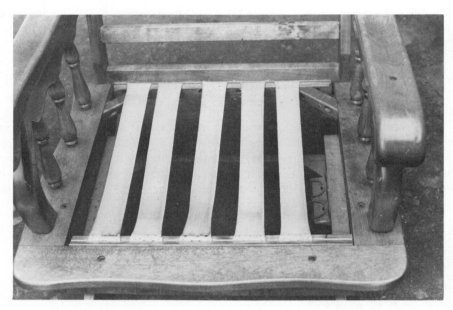

156.   Loose cushion seat with rubber webbing strips.

Rubber webbing in a short time sags with use and dries out from heat.

Dried out or weak webbing should be replaced with new webbing. Rubber webbing and clips, which are sold in upholstery shops, are very easy to install; any salesman can tell you how to install them. If you wish to change the support of the seat, it is wiser to replace rubber webbing with upholstery webbing as in illustration 157.

157.   Upholstery webbing used to replace rubber webbing.

V. Seats with Steel Bars

On some chairs with a small seat opening, steel bars are installed on which coil springs are mounted. If the coil spring is broken, replace it with a good one; and if the steel bar is too weak and sags, repair it with steel webbing as in illustration 158. If you cannot repair it this way, install upholstery webbing with coil springs.

158.   Installing steel webbing. Repairing steel bars.

Step 9

THE WINGS (Inside)

(a)   On some chairs or sofas you would first cover the wings before covering the arms (see illustration 159).

(b)   On other chairs or sofas you would first cover the arms before covering the wings (see illustration 160).

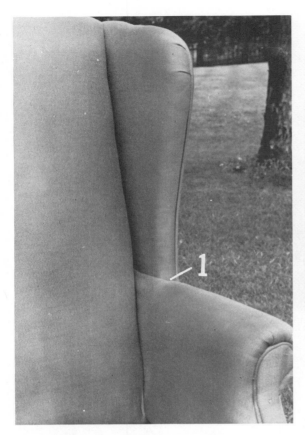

159. Wings are covered before covering the arms.

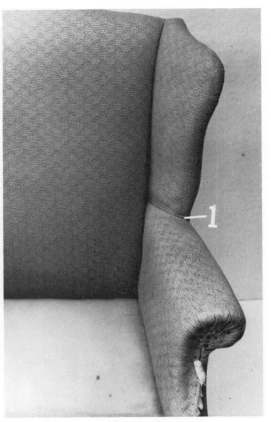

160. Arms are covered before covering the wings.

To determine which procedure to follow to finish the wings and arms, you must first look at the way your chair or sofa wings were covered before. If the joint (1) between the arm and the wing is finished by the wing (that is, the wing covers the arm at this joint), do the arm first. If the joint is finished by the arm, do the wing first.

Self-cording is encased cord in a folded edge of a piece of fabric.

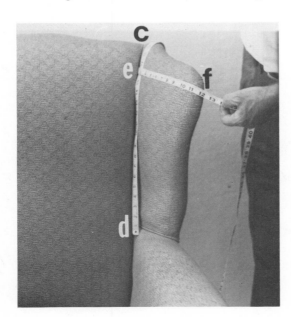

1. See illustration 161. Measure the inside wing length—(c) to (d), plus a 3″ allowance for handling.

2. Measure inside wing width—(e) to (f), plus a 3″ allowance for handling.

3. Cut two matching (in dimension and pattern) pieces according to the measurements.

161. Taking measurements for the wing.

4. On the bottom of the wing covers make self-cording (g) and cut an opening (h) to fit on the back top rail (see illustration 162).

5. Put the wing cover in place. Place the self-cording (g) along the joint with the arm and tack it at the bottom to the outside of the wing. Now pull the bottom (cording) edge of the wing cover tightly and push the side (s) between the back post and the back tacking strip, and tack outside to the back post. Pull the top of the wing cover (t) over the top of the wing and tack to the outside of the wing rail, making sure the pattern is straight. Pull the front side of the wing cover (k) tightly and tack to the outside of the wing post.

Note: The above steps are for covering the wings after the arms. For covering the wings first, repeat the above steps but omit the welting cord. Tack the bottom of the wing cover to the arm rail. Then the arm cover will finish the joint with the wing.

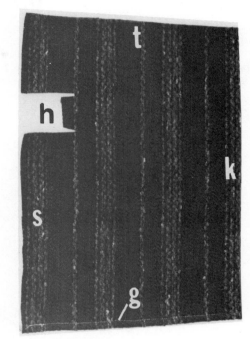

162.   Right wing cover.

Step 10

THE ARMS (Inside)

The frame of the arms consists of arm rails (a), arm posts (b), back posts (c), and tacking strips (d) (see illustration 163). For a base for the arm frames, use webbing covered with burlap and padded with filling.

163.   Frame of the arm.

On small arm openings, instead of webbing use sagless (see illustration 164). Sagless is a tightly webbed material similar to burlap. It is the best material for covering small openings on seats, arms, and backs for base support. For padding, you can use a variety of fillings. For padding use cotton, foam rubber, or both. If you use upholstery cotton for padding, put two or three layers about 2″ to 3″ thick total, depending on how thick and fluffy you wish to build. Spread the cotton smoothly so that it covers the entire arm, then cover with muslin to keep the padding in place.

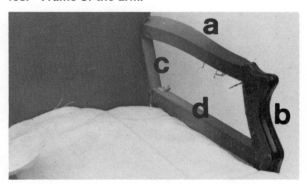

Note: Always cover wooden edges with a layer of cotton or 1/2″ layer of foam rubber to prevent wearing out the final cover. For this reason and for a smooth finish in front of the arm, install an edge roll.

164.   Covering the small arm opening with sagless for support of finished arm.

Final Cover

The inside arm cover is tacked to the frame on all four sides. Chair and sofa arms vary in construction, shape, and feel. Thus, many arms require their own particular work. To simplify matters so that you can understand the main principle of installing the final cover on the arms, I will classify the arms into six main groups:

165.

I. Open Padded Arms

Some are padded and covered from the front to the back of the arm as in illustration 165. The front of the cover is blind-tacked, the back is tacked in back to the back post, and the sides are tacked to the bottom of the arm rails.

166.

Other arms have part of the top arm padded and covered as in illustration 166. Some are padded on separate wooden panels and bolted to the top of the arm. To recover, take off the padded part, recover, and put it back in place.

II.   Swept Arms

See illustration 167. The top of the arm is curved from the front of the chair (a) or sofa to the top of the back (b). Swept arms cannot be covered in one piece.

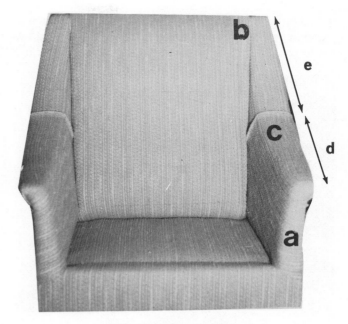

167.   Swept arm chair.

The arm cover should be done from two pieces sewn together as in illustrations 167–169, or tacked together as in illustrations 172 and 173.

1.   See illustration 168. Measure the front part of the arm (f), at the widest points only. Take two pieces that match in dimension and pattern and cut according to the measurements for the left and right arms.

168.   Two pieces of the arm cover sewn together.

2. Measure the back part of the arm (g), at the widest points only, and cut two matching pieces (in dimension and pattern) for both arms. These pieces should match the front part of the arm cover in pattern as in illustration 169.

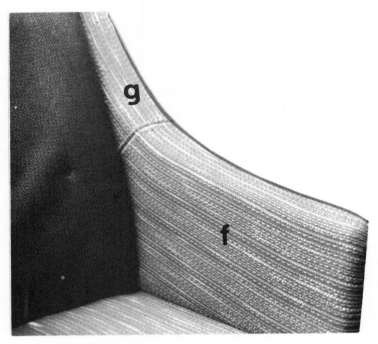

169. Matching pattern on the front (f) and back (g) arm cover.

3. On the bottom of the back part of the arm cover, make self-cording and place temporarily on the arm as in illustration 170.

4. Temporarily place the front part of the arm cover on the arm and over the cording. Mark a chalk line for the seam as in illustration 171.

170. Placing, temporarily, back part of the arm cover.

171. Marking chalk line for the seam.

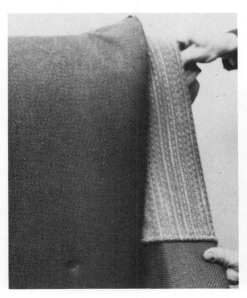

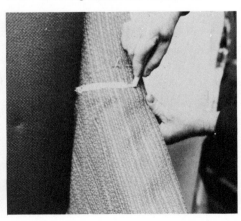

5.   Take off the front and back arm covers and sew the back-piece cording to the front piece along the chalk line to make one arm-cover piece.

6.   Place the arm cover on the arm, and tack each side to the frame. The finished project will look like illustration 169.

COVERING SWEPT ARM WITH TACKING

See illustration 172. The inside arm cover consists of two pieces: the inside arm cover (h) and the top (k) with front (n) arm cover, which are tacked together.

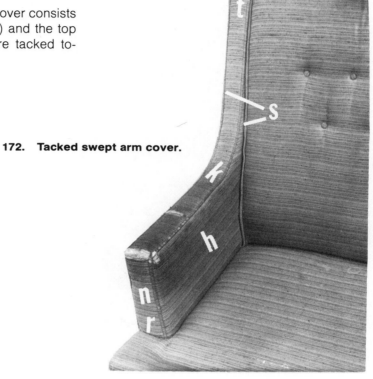

172.   Tacked swept arm cover.

1.   Measure the length of the top and front of the arm cover, from top (t) to bottom (r), and add 3″ for handling.

2.   Measure the arm width between cording seams (s), and add 1″ to each side for tacking to the frame.

3.   Cut two matching pieces, in dimension and pattern, one for the left arm and one for the right arm, and tack to the arm on both sides.

4.   Make four pieces of cording, two for each arm, of the length measured in step 1 and tack to the frame, one inside and one outside of each arm along the arm edges.

5.   Lay the chair on its side, place the fabric over the outside arm, and trace all around the arm edges with chalk onto the fabric. Add 1 1/2″ to this border all the way around. Make midpoint marks on the top arm cover and on the top of the arm to center the arm cover for blind tacking.

6. Make sure the pattern on the left arm and right arm matches, and cut two pieces for the inside arms and similarly cut out two pieces for the outside arms.

Note: Inside and outside arm covers on the swept arms have the same dimensions.

7. Install inside arm covers with blind tacking on the top with tacking tape and in front with a metal tacking strip or by sewing with blind stitching to the front inside arm edge. The back is tacked to the back post and the bottom to the side seat railing.

173. **Swept arm chair.**

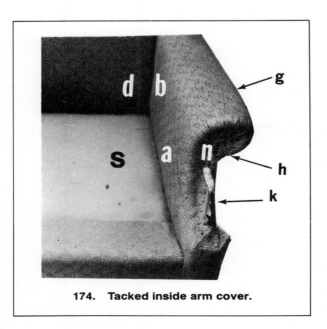

174. **Tacked inside arm cover.**

III. Curved Arms

See illustration 174. The four sides of the final cover should be tacked to the frame: the bottom of the arm cover (a) should be tacked to the side seat rail, pushing between the seat (s) and the arm. The back of the arm cover (b) should be tacked to the back post, pushing between back (d) and the arm. The top of the arm cover (g) should be tacked to the outside under the arm rail (h). This can be seen more clearly in illustration 175. The front of the arm cover (n) should be tacked to the front of the arm post (k). On some curved arms you will install welting cord (m) all around the front of the arm edge as in illustration 176 and install the arm panel (p) as in illustration 177. A third variation is to install the cording on the edge of the front arm (n) without an arm panel as in illustration 178.

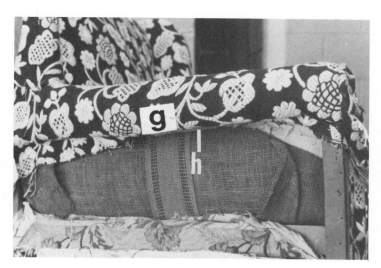

175. The top of the inside arm cover (g) is tacked to the outside, under the arm rail (h).

176. Cording around the front arm edge.

177. Arm with arm panel.

178. Finished front arm without an arm panel.

1. See illustration 178. Trim off the front arm cover (n) and cording (r).

179.   Installed front arm cover.

2.   Take measurements of the front arm, widest points only, add 2″ (total), cut two matching front arm covers (for the left and right arms) from your upholstery fabric, and install on the front arm as in illustration 179, using staples or tacks.

3.   Measure along the arm as in illustration 180 for welting cord measurements, add 3″ total and make two welting cords.

4.   See illustration 179. Measure for the arm covers from the bottom (s) of the arm front to the outside bottom (t) of the arm rail, following the inside front arm edge, and from the front arm edge (v) to the back arm post (w) add (total) 3″ for handling.

5.   Cut two matching inside arm covers (one for each arm) from your upholstery fabric.

6.   Sew the cording to the front end of the arm cover as in illustration 181.

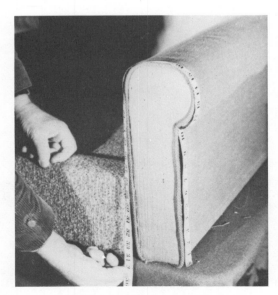

180.   Measurement for the length of the cording.

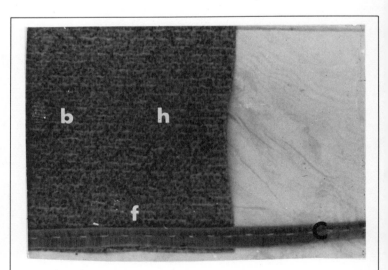

b — bottom of arm cover
c — loose part of cording
f — front of arm cover
h — arm cover

181.   Cording sewn to the arm cover.

7.   See illustration 182. Blind-tack the arm cover (x) with the cording to the inside and top arm edge, using tacking tape, and tack the loose part of the cording (c) to the outside arm edge, using staples or tacks.

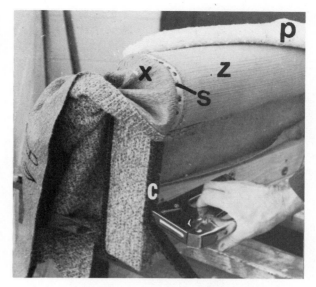

182.   Installing the arm cover and cording.

8.   Put some padding (p) (cotton) on the arm (z) to make it even with the cording seam (s).

9.   Tack the arm cover to the frame.

The completed front and inside arm are shown in illustration 183.

183.   Completed arm.

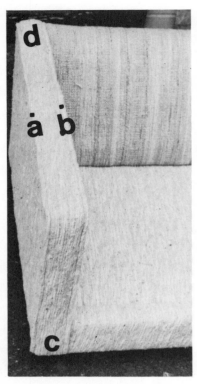

184. Closed boxed arm.

IV. Closed Boxed Arms

The main distinction in boxed arms is that the front arm post and top arm railing have the same width. Arm openings inside and outside are covered with hard cardboard. Illustration 185 shows the inside of the arm covered with cardboard, and the outside is done similarly. Both are covered with one layer of cotton padding. The top of the arm should be padded with two layers of cotton.

1. See illustration 184. Take a measurement for the boxing width between the arm edges (a) and (b). Add 1 1/4″ on each side for self-cording.

2. Measure the length of the boxing from the front of the arm at the bottom (c) to the back of the arm (d), and add 3″ for handling.

3. Cut two matching pieces, in dimension and pattern, one for the left arm and one for the right arm.

4. Make self-cording on each side of the boxing. The exact dimension between the cording seams should be the same as the dimension between the arm edges (a) and (b).

5. Put the boxing on the arm and make chalk marks at the corners as in illustration 185.

6. See illustration 185. Measure the outside of the arm from the front (e) to the back (f) and from the top (g) to the bottom (h), widest points only. Add 1 1/2″ to each side for handling.

185. Marking the corners.

7. Cut, as per dimensions, two matching pieces for the inside arm covers and two matching pieces for the outside arm covers and mark sewing lines (k) on finish side as in illustration 186.

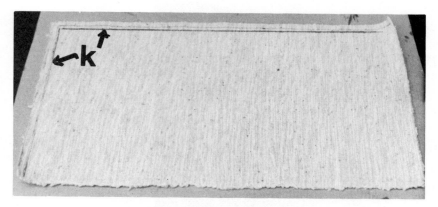

186.   Marked sewing lines.

8. Sew the boxing to the inside arm cover, starting from the corner in any direction, to the end, then move the zipper foot to the other side and finish sewing in the other direction from the same corner to the other end (see illustration 187).

187.   Boxing sewed to the top of the arm cover.

188. Arm casing.

9. Sew the same boxing to the outside arm cover the same way as you did the inside arm cover. The finished project would be the arm casing (see illustration 188).

189. Sliding the arm casing over the arm.

10. In the same way make a casing for the other arm.

11. Slide the arm casing over the arm as in illustration 189 and tack to the frame.

The final cover is prepared as in illustration 188 and installed in one piece to cover the whole arm (top, front, and both sides).

V. Arm with Exposed Wood

It is easy to cover an arm made of exposed wood. Cover a small arm opening, for support, with sagless. For a large arm opening, install webbing, then cover with burlap. Pad firmly with cotton or foam, cover with muslin, then install the final cover.

All work will be done on the inside of the arm and on the top of the arm. Illustration 190, looking from outside the arm, shows sagless and padding, covered with muslin. If the old arm is good, cover with a new cover.

190. Inside arm padded and covered with muslin.

1. See illustration 191. Measure the arm from the arm post, widest point only (a), to the back post, pushing the tape measure between the arm (b) and the back (c).

2. See illustrations 190 and 191. Measure from the side seat rail (r), pushing the tape measure between the back (b) and seat (s) to the outside arm rail (d) as in illustration 190. The white line (r) shows the location of the top edge of the side seat rail.

3. Cut two pieces of cover material, as per dimensions, so that one arm cover matches the pattern of the other arm cover.

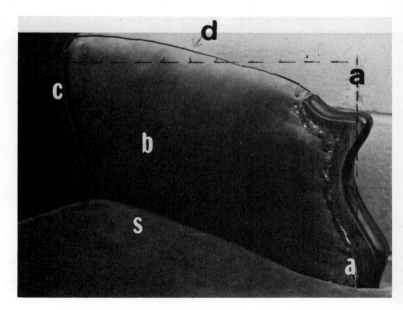

191. Inside arm cover installed.

4. Tack the bottom of the arm cover to the side seat rail (r) (see illustration 190). The back of the cover is tacked to the back post after pulling it between the arm and the back. The top is tacked to the outside arm rail (d) and the front of the cover is tacked to the arm post, close to the finished part of the exposed wood. Then trim off excess cover material as in illustration 191.

5. See illustration 192. Now finish the edge close to the exposed wood. On old-fashioned projects, finish with gimp (1) or upholstery nails (2), and on modern projects, double cording (3).

Finishing the arm edges close to the exposed wood is done the same way as for seats with exposed wood.

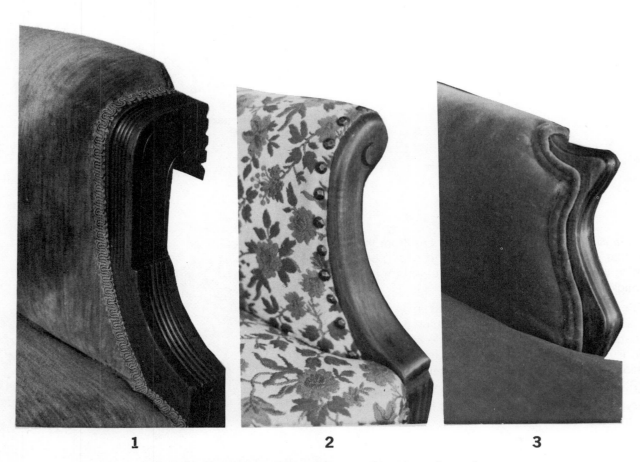

1   **2**   **3**

192.   Finished arm edges close to the exposed wood.

VI.   T-Arms

T-arm cover consists of three pieces: the top arm cover (a), welt cording (b), and inside arm cover (c) as in illustration 193 or two pieces without welt cording. To describe how to cover a T-arm, we will continue covering a piped-back wing chair, which we started on page 51, illustration 92. We have installed the seat cover previously.

193.   Piped-back wing chair.

1.   Take measurements for the top arm cover as in illustration 194. Add 1″ to each side for handling.

2.   Cut two matching pieces, in dimension and pattern, one for the left arm and one for the right arm.

194.   Measuring for the top arm cover.

3. Install the top arm cover as in illustration 195.

Note: Cut off cording as in illustration 196 before installing the top arm cover.

195. Installed top arm cover and measurements for the inside wing cover.

196. Cutting the cording off.

4.   Install inside wing cover as in illustration 197.

197. Installed top arm and inside wing covers, and measurements for the inside back.

5.   See illustration 198. Measure the inside arm cover, starting in the front from the arm post (outside) (d) to the back post, pushing the tape measure between the arm (e) and the back (f). Add 3″ total for handling.

6.   Measure from the arm cording (g) to the side arm rail, pushing the tape measure between the seat (h) and arm (e).

7.   Cut two pieces of cover material, as per dimensions, so that the arm cover matches the pattern of the other arm cover.

8.   Cut two strips for cording 2″ wide and as long as the dimension for the inside arm cover, from the front to the back. Cut one for each arm.

198. Measurements for the inside arm cover.

9. Install cording as in illustration 199.

199. Installed cording.

200. Blind tacking the inside arm cover.

10. Blind-tack the inside arm cover (m) as in illustration 200.

11. Pull down the inside arm cover and tack completely to the frame (see illustration 201).

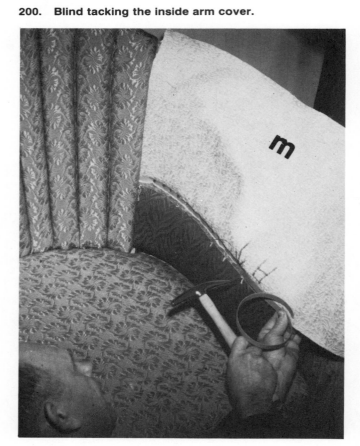

201. Completed inside chair.

Covering Inside Arms: An Overview

See illustrations 202 and 203. To install the final cover for any arm of a chair or sofa, follow one main principle; the top and front of the arm will be finished differently, but the bottom and the back of the arm covers will be installed the same way for most styles. All four sides of the final cover are tacked to the frame. The top of the cover (k) is installed to the arm rail (a), the difference depending on the style of the arm.

The front of the cover (p) is tacked to the arm post (b), and will differ depending on the arm style. The bottom of the cover (a), for most arm styles, is tacked to the side seat rail (c) (outside). The back of cover is tacked to the back post (d); however, part of (e) is tacked over the back top arm rail, outside the back post (g). Part (f) is installed between the side back tacking strip (o) and the back post (d), above the bottom back tacking strip (s). Part (n) should be installed between the tacking strip (s) and the back seat rail (t) to the back post (d).

opening for back post

opening for bottom tacking strip

opening for back seat rail

opening for arm post

202. Final arm cover for left arm.

203. Frame of the arm.

204. Webbing is installed on the back.

Step 11

THE BACK (Inside)

After completing the seat and arms, start working on the back. This work repeats the processes used on the seat and arms.

I. Webbing

If the webbing is not good but the springs are not broken and are tied well, new webbing can be applied over the old webbing. Otherwise, remove the old back, including the springs and webbing, and install new webbing the same way as on the seat but not as close together as on the seat (see illustration 204).

205. Back completed to cover with burlap.

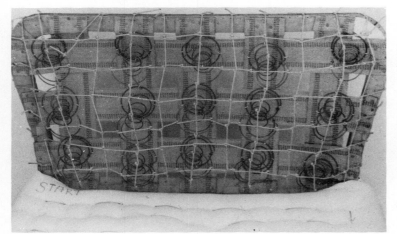

II. The Springs

The springs on the back are not as heavy (coil springs) as on the seat. Sew each spring to the webbing as described for the seat. For rounded edges, do as for a rounded seat, and for square edges, do as for a flat seat. Sew one spring on each webbing intersection. Then tie the springs with spring twine, from top to bottom, side to side, and between rows of the springs. Diagonal tying is not necessary because there is less need for support than on the seat (see illustration 205).

For the back support, zigzag springs are most commonly used as in illustration 206 or a steel bar with springs is used. To make the support stronger and smoother, support the back with zigzag springs, refine them the same way as on the seat (see illustration 153, page 72). Cover the springs with burlap.

206.　Zigzag springs on the back.

III.　Padding

The back is more thickly padded than any other part of a chair or sofa if the back does not have loose cushions. If the back has loose cushions, the back is padded very thinly. The padding for the back is of the same materials as on the seat or arms. For smoothness, comfort, and good appearance, put a 1/2″ layer of polyfoam over the cotton or other loose fiber. If you do not use a layer of foam, cover the padding with muslin.

Note:　When installing all back supports such as webbing, spring twine, burlap, and muslin, secure to the back tacking strips *only*, unless there are none on the frame. When installing the final cover, it can then be pushed around the tacking strips.

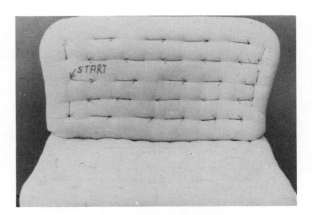

207.　Tufted back.

IV.　Tufting the Back Down

When the padding is completed and covered with muslin, it is better to tuft the back down as in illustration 207. For instructions, see ''Tufting the Seat Down,'' pages 48–49.

208. Cutting opening for fitting.

V. Final Cover

The final cover of the inside back may consist of a one-piece back cover (a) as in illustration 208 or a back cover (a) with a border (b) as in illustration 209.

A. COVERING INSIDE BACK IN ONE PIECE

1. Measure the width of the back, widest points only, side to side, from the back post on one side to the back post on the other side. Push the tape measure between the arm and the back on both sides for this measurement.

2. Measure the height of the back from the top back rail (outside) to the back seat rail (also outside), pushing the tape measure between the seat and the back.

3. Cut, in rectangular form, the upholstery fabric according to the measurements.

4. Mark the midpoint marks on the top of the back rail (outside), back seat rail (outside), and the top and bottom of the back cover.

5. Lay the back cover on the back of your project in position so that the midpoint marks on the back cover line up with midpoint marks on the back frame, and tack the cover temporarily on the top and bottom.

6. Cut openings on the top for fitting the corners at the joints of the back posts and back top rail as in illustration 208. Also cut openings on the bottom for fitting in the corners, joining the back posts and bottom tacking strip. The back cover prepared for installation is shown in illustration 210.

209. Taking measurements for the back cover.

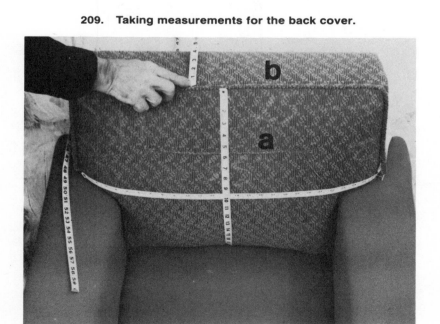

7. See illustration 208. Sides (s) should be pushed between the arms and the back and tacked to the back post. The top is tacked to the top back rail (outside) and the bottom is pushed between the back and seat and is tacked to the back seat rail (outside).

210. One-piece final back cover.

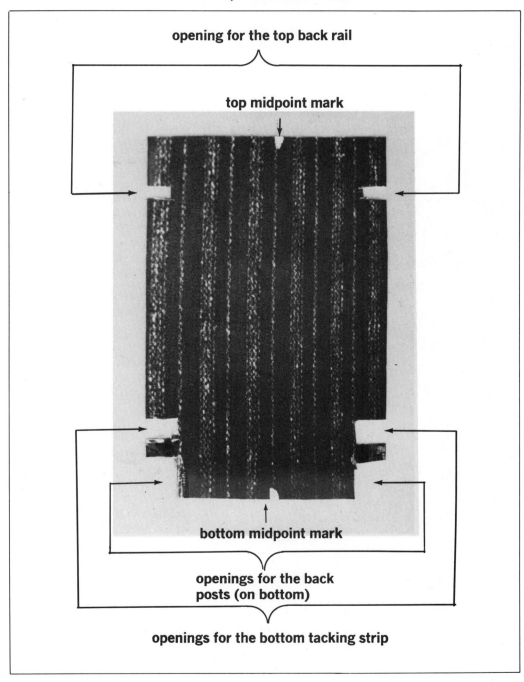

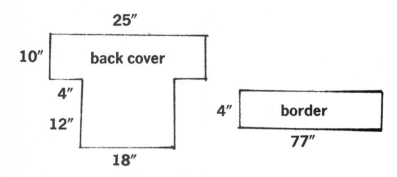

211. Paper plan for back cover with border.

B. BACK COVER WITH A BORDER SEWED TO THE BACK COVER

See illustration 209. The final back cover with a border will be made completely before installation.

1. Make a paper plan as in illustration 211 and put on the dimensions from the measurements of the back. In this example the exact dimensions are as shown on the paper plan.

212. Marked back cover.

2. On upholstery fabric, mark the sewing lines (f) according to the measurements. Make a 1″ border (h) around the sewing lines (these are the cutting lines).

3. Cut out from your fabric the back cover in rectangle form as in illustration 212 and cut off excess (x).

4. Mark the midpoint marks on the top and bottom of the back cover.

213. Measurement for length of border.

5. Measure the length of the border from side (c) to side (g) as in illustration 213. Add 2″ on each end for handling.

6. Measure the width of the border as in illustration 209 from the cording seam in front to the outside edge of the back rail. Add a total of 3″: 1 1/2″ for self-cording (in front) and 1 1/2″ in back of the border for tacking to the frame.

7. Cut, from your fabric, the border as per your measurements.

8. In front of the border, make self-cording.

9. Make a midpoint mark on the border, making sure the pattern on the border and back cover matches, and mark each corner as in illustration 214.

214. Marked back cover with border and stretcher.

10. Under presser foot of the sewing machine, lay the back cover, finish side up. On top of the back cover, lay the border, also finish side up.

11. Join midpoint marks of the top back cover and border, then start with narrow stitches to sew the border to the back cover so that the seam of the cording lies directly on the sewing chalk mark of the back cover.

12. As you come to the first corner mark on the border, turn the corner and continue sewing the border to the back cover along the chalk line to the next corner. Then turn the corner and continue similarly until the border is completely sewn to the back cover (in one direction from midpoint marks).

Note: Use border as a guide for turning corners since the back cover may possibly stretch and give a larger measurement than needed. To turn a corner the machine should be stopped while the needle is in the material you are sewing. Lift the presser foot and turn the material in the direction you are sewing, while the needle acts as the axis. Lower the presser foot and start to sew.

13. After you have finished sewing the border to the back cover in one direction from the midpoint marks, move the zipper-foot attachment to the other side and start to sew from the midpoint marks in the opposite direction.

14. Remove the old back cover with the border from your project.

15. Place the new back cover with the border on the back of your project, cut necessary openings on the border for fitting, and tack to the frame.

215.   Quilted back.

C.   QUILTED BACK

Quilt is a cover made of two layers of cloth filled with down, cotton, wool, or other soft material, and stitched together in a pattern. A quilted back is made for decorative purposes and variety. Quilted finishing can be installed not only on the back but on all parts of furniture pieces. For this purpose buy a quilted upholstery fabric. To make a new quilted cover, cut from the fabric the back cover per dimensions, then cut the same size piece of muslin and a piece of foam about 1/8″ or 1/2″ thick. Thicker foam makes deeper seams. Mark, with chalk, the desired pattern on the finishing side of the back cover. Under the back cover lay a piece of foam, then muslin. Baste these three pieces together, following the lines (pattern lines), then sew with a sewing machine over the basted lines. After finishing, you will get a one-piece quilted back cover. Install on the back of your project. Quilting can be done in many different sizes and patterns such as squares or diamonds. If the old back cover is already quilted as in illustration 215, you may cover the old quilted back cover with a new fabric.

216.   Removing the quilted back cover.

1.   Take off the old back cover as in illustration 216.

2.   Cut a piece of your upholstery fabric, 2″ (total), larger than the old back cover.

3.   Lay the new back cover on top of the old one and baste to the old cover, following the quilted pattern lines. Then sew the lines with a sewing machine. You will get a quilted back cover like the one in illustration 217.

4. The finished quilted back is installed on the back of your project by the same method used for any back cover.

5. Install buttons.

217.   Quilted back cover.

D.   PIPED OR CHANNELED BACK

   This is made for decorative purposes and variety. Piped-back furniture is more expensive as it takes more time to make. For covering piped pieces of furniture, you should select a fabric that has no pattern or a small pattern that will fall evenly. A piped back is installed in one piece (piped cushion). In front of the piped cushion is a final cover; on the other side (in the back of the cushion) is muslin or a similar material. The final material and muslin are sewn together between the channels. For installing the final cover on the small and thinly piped back, it is better to remove the back (piped cushion), put the final cover over the back, baste between the channels, and then sew over with a sewing machine, starting from the center and then going to the sides. The finished piped cushion is installed on the back of your project the same way as it was initially installed. You do not need to remove a heavily padded piped back from your project. You can install the final cover over the old one. For clarity, we will cover the piped back on the piped-back wing chair (see page 51).

1. See illustration 218. Measure width, widest points only, from the side (a) to the side (b), measuring with the tape measure over the channels and down to the seams, then add 4″ (total) for handling.

2. Measure the height from the back seat rail, pushing the tape measure between the back (c) and the seat (d) to the top back rail (e) (outside). Add 4″ (total) for handling (see illustration 218).

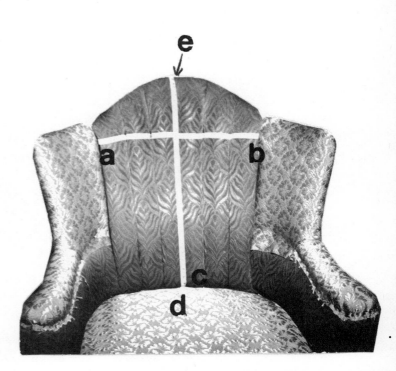

218.   Measurements.

3. Cut, from your fabric, the back cover as per your measurements, and put midpoint marks on the top and bottom of the back cover.

4. Lay the back cover on the back of your project in position so that the midpoint marks line up in the center, on the top and bottom of the back. The top of the cover is tacked to the top back rail (outside) and the bottom is tacked to the back seat rail, pushing the cover between the back and seat.

5. Sew, by hand, the final cover to the back, to the seam between channels as in illustration 219. With a matching color of thread, make short stitches in front of the back and 1″–2″ long stitches on the back side.

219. Installing the back cover.

6. After you finish sewing one row of the channels, in the center, do the next one. Tack on the top and bottom, and sew to the old seam as above. Work from the center to the sides, sewing all seams after tacking. For fitting the bottom of the cover, it is cut as in illustration 220. All rounded backs are done this way.

220. Cutting the bottom of the inside back cover for fitting.

7. See illustration 221. Cut openings in the final cover, for fitting, on the top (t) for the back top rail and on the bottom (b) for the bottom tacking strip. Push side (s) between the back and the arm with wing (arm wing) and tack to the back post. The top (t) is folded underneath the last (outside) channel and tacked to the back top rail. The bottom (b) is pulled under the back tacking strip and tacked to the back seat rail outside.

After sewing the final cover between channels and tacking to the frame, your piped back will be finished.

221.   Cutting an opening for fitting.

E.   DIAMOND-TUFTED BACK

Deep diamond tufting is used on decorative furniture pieces and to secure padding by means of regularly spaced tufts. For diamond tufting, you must have deep grooves in the padding where the pleats will lie. The grooves are between buttons, which are on the diamond corners in deep punched holes (see illustration 222). Diamond-tufted patterns of the cover are made by pulling buttons deeply into the back padding and joining them with deep pleats. Buttons hold the pleats in their proper locations. For a diamond-tufted back, you should select a fabric the same as for the piped back, without a pattern or with a pattern that will spread evenly.

222.   Foam padding for a diamond-tufted back.

1. Measure the back of your project, the side to the side and from the back seat rail to the top back rail outside, widest points only. Add (total) 2″ plus 2″ for each groove or to each button location.

2. Cut the back cover from your upholstery fabric as per dimensions.

3. Cut off the old buttons and remove the old back cover.

4. Place the new back cover on the back of your project and tack temporarily, centering the top and bottom of the final cover.

5. Thread a straight 8″ long needle with sewing twine. Start at the center of the buttons and insert the needle from outside through the back and new cover in the place where there was a button before. Make a 1/8″ stitch on the new cover and push the needle back to the outside back, pull the twine tightly, and secure with a knot.

6. Work from the center and do similarly the next button places. Between the button places the cover will be folded in the grooves.

7. From each outside button place, make a fold, pull tight, and tack to the frame.

8. Install buttons.

Step 12

THE BUTTONS

Buttons are installed on many pieces of furniture. On most pieces they are on the back of the furniture but on some they are also on the seat and arms. These are used mainly for decorative purposes. Other purposes are to hold the cover in place, as on barrel backs and tufted surfaces, and to hold the padding in place, as some backs are filled with crushed foam or feathers.

The sizes of the buttons differ but the most popular sizes are #22 (the size of a dime), used for diamond tufting, #30 (the size of a nickel), mostly used on rounded backs to hold the cover and/or padding in place; #36 (the size of a quarter), mostly used for decorative purposes. Button shells are enclosed by a button machine. Buttons may be covered in any upholstery shop. Illustration 223 shows encased buttons of the three popular sizes.

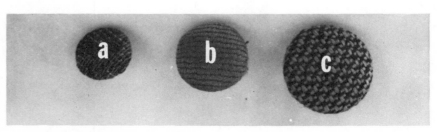

223. **Three popular sizes of buttons.** a) #22 b) #30
c) #36 **Shown actual size.**

    Installing the buttons: see illustrations 224 and 225. Use a straight needle long enough to go through the back of your project (8″–10″) and very strong sewing twine. Twine must be long enough to pass, double, through all the padding, and enough for making a knot outside the back.

1.   Thread the twine into the loop of the button.

2.   Insert both ends of the twine through the eye of the needle, put both ends of twine through the back, using the needle.

3.   Tie the twine tightly, placing a piece of any material between the back and the slipknot. After pulling the slipknot tightly, make double overhand knots to secure permanently.

Note: If the button is not deep enough because of thin padding, after you have finished tying the button pull the sewing twine tightly and secure to the frame as in illustration 227.

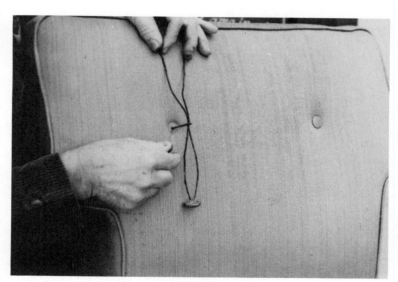

The number of buttons installed is a matter of personal taste.

224.

225. Installing the buttons.

226. Back view of the completed buttons tied to the back.

227. Twine secured to the frame to pull the button deep into the back padding.

Step 13

THE CUSHION

The cushion is a soft pad that fits into the seat of a chair or sofa for comfort. The filling determines the comfort, life, and looks of a cushion. Common materials used for fillings are foam rubber, and inner springs encased in burlap, padded with cotton for softness and form. Foam rubber is more durable and is much more commonly used. Cushion forms vary from rectangular to oval and round shapes as in illustration 228, already encased. The most common thickness is 4″ but other size cushions are found.

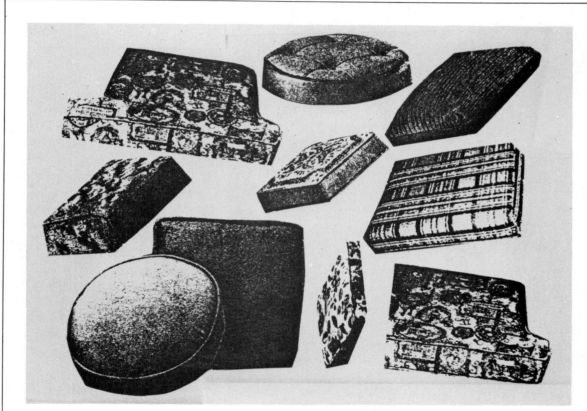

228.   Encased cushion forms.

The upholstered cushion consists of two parts: cushion and casing.

a)   The cushion is the uncovered foam rubber or inner spring padded form. If the old cushion is not good, replace it with a new foam one, 1/2″ longer and wider for each foot than the seam-to-seam casing measurement of the old one. For example: for a casing 24″ x 24″ x 3 3/4″, the foam cushion should measure 25″ x 25″ x 4″.

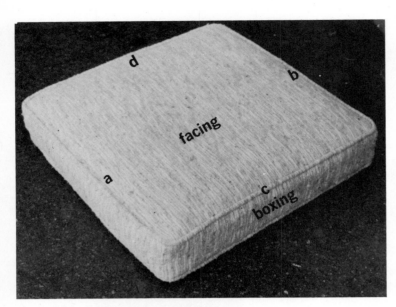

229. Boxed cushion (rectangular form).

b) The casing is the cover for the cushion.

Boxed Cushion

The casing for a boxed cushion consists of two facings and a boxing.

Preparing the Casing for a 4″-Thick Cushion

I. Rectangular Form (Boxed Cushion)
Measurements and Cutting

1. Make a paper plan and code it. Bx—boxing, CF—cushion facing.

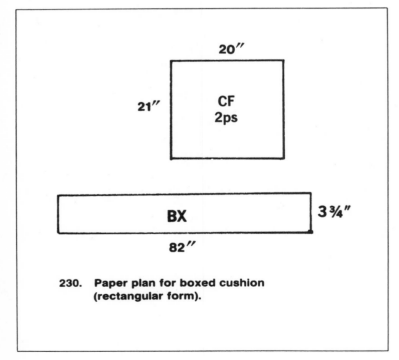

230. Paper plan for boxed cushion (rectangular form).

2. If the cushion is firm and fits well on the seat, take the measurements from the cushion casing, measuring from the cording seam in all directions. Put your dimensions on the paper plan. For example, see illustration 229, side (a) to side (b) is 20″ and front (c) to back (d) is 21″. Mark as shown on the paper plan in illustration 230. Add the four dimensions to give a total that is the length of the boxing, which in the example is 82″. Thus, the exact measurements are 20″ x 21″ for each of the two facings and 3 3/4″ x 82″ for the boxing.

3. On the finishing side of the upholstery fabric, mark with chalk lines for the two facings 20″ x 21″, which will be sewing lines. Make a 1″ border around the outside for the seams. For the boxing 3 3/4″ x 82″, add 1″ on each end for the seam and 1 1/4″ on each side for self-cording. In this example your cutting dimensions would be a 22″ x 23″ piece for each facing (2) and a 6 1/4″ x 84″ piece for the boxing.

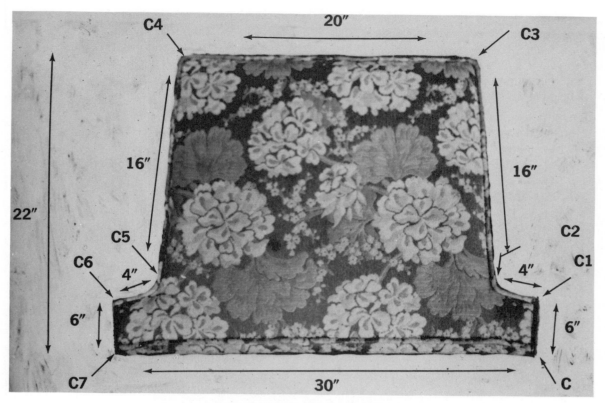

231. T-form (boxed cushion).

II. T-Form Style

1. Make a paper plan.

2. Make measurements from the widest points of the cushion and put these dimensions on your paper plan. For this example the widest points of the cushion are 30″ side to side and 22″ from front to back. Now take the cushion measurements C-C1 (6″), C1-C2 (4″), C2-C3 (16″). Same dimensions for the other side. The back C3-C4 is 20″. The front C-C7 is 30″. Put these on your paper plan as in illustration 232.

3. Add all dimensions around your T-form cushion facing to give a total equal to the boxing length (102″).

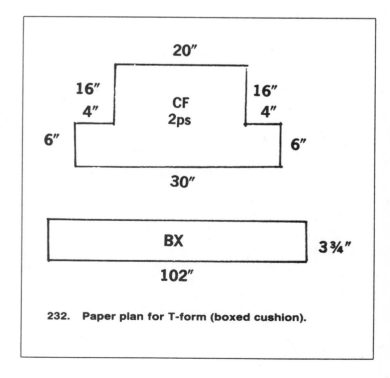

232. Paper plan for T-form (boxed cushion).

4. See illustration 233. Transfer these dimensions from your paper plan to your upholstery fabric (finish side). These lines are again your sewing lines. Make a 1″ border around the entire T-form facings for the seam; this outside line is your cutting edge. Cut the facings out first in rectangular form and then remove (x). For example, these facings would require a cut rectangle 24″ x 32″ before removing (x). Snip corners (c) to about 1/4″ of the sewing line.

Transfer boxing dimensions to the upholstery fabric. For the boxing (3 3/4″ x 102″) add 1″ on each end for the seam and 1 1/4″ on each side for self-cording. In this example your cutting dimensions for the boxing would be 6 1/4″ x 104″.

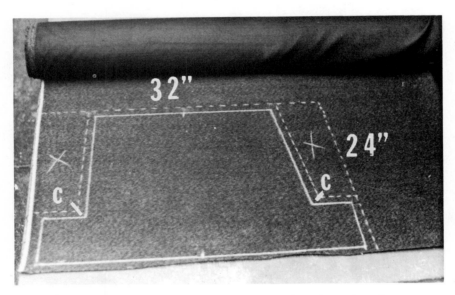

233. Marked lines for T-form cushion facing. The solid white line is the sewing line. The dotted line around the sewing line is the cutting line for the final cover. X is excess material.

III. Measurements for Other Forms (Round, Oval, Etc.)

It is not easy to take measurements for a casing from a cushion or seat that does not have rectilinear (straight-line) edges. Many upholstery instructors recommend the use of the old cover as a pattern but do not say what you should do if the casing is not good enough to use as a pattern or has been thrown away. No matter how good your old casing is, *do not* use it as a pattern since material stretches and changes shape with use.

The easiest way to take measurements for a cushion casing is to make a pattern on the chair seat with hard paper. Follow the steps shown in illustrations 234 and 235. This is an example for a piped-back wing chair (see page 51).

1. Make midpoint marks, with chalk, on the front-seat edge (e) and back seat (f). You may put the mark on the bottom of the back (f) as in illustration 234.

2. Cut a piece of hard paper just a little larger than half the chair seat.

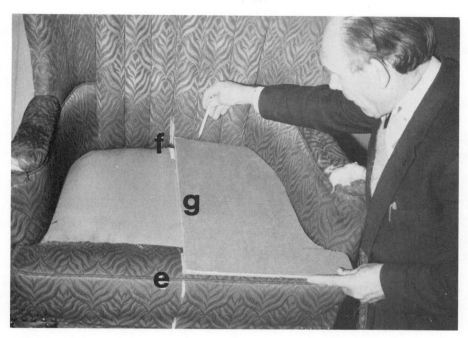

234.

3.   Put the paper on the seat so that the midpoint marks (e) and (f) are connected with a straight-edge side (g) of the paper (see illustration 234).

4.   Cut the other sides of the paper for a perfect fit for half the seat.

5.   Cut a duplicate of the paper for the other half of the seat, then join the two halves (g) and (h) together with tape. You have just made a pattern for the entire seat-cushion facing, which is hard and will not change shape with handling (see illustration 235).

235.   The pattern on the seat for fitting.

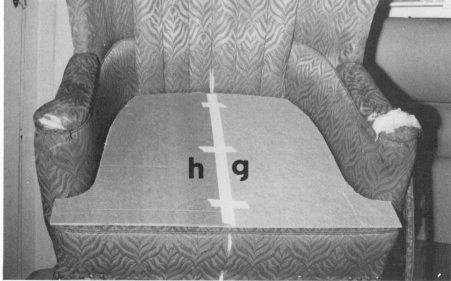

6. Put the pattern on the seat and recheck for fit. Correct by cutting or patching with hard paper. Do not make the pattern too tight since there should be about 1/8″ clearance on all sides.

7. Put the pattern on the finishing side of the fabric as in illustration 236, make a chalk sewing line all around the pattern, make a 1″ border around this sewing line for the seam, and cut out as in illustration 237. Repeat for the other facing.

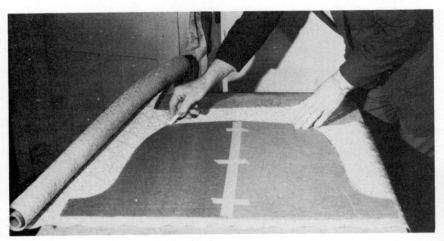

236. Marking a chalk sewing line all around the pattern.

237. Cutting the pattern out in rectangular form. Note: The solid white line is the sewing line, while the dotted line around this is the cutting line for the final cover. X is excess material.

8. Measure the distance with a tape measure around the pattern sew lines. This is the length for your boxing; add 2″ for the seam, 1 1/4″ on top, and 1 1/4″ on bottom for self-cording.

Final Preparation

FACINGS

1. On the finishing side of your facings, in front, make a midpoint mark with chalk. On nonrectangular forms, make a midpoint mark in front and back, and on oval or rounded forms, front, back, and side midpoint marks are needed for symmetrical joining of the facings to the boxing.

2. On the reverse side of your facings, make arrows indicating the direction they will lie on your project and code them (CF—Cushion facing) for indentification.

BOXING (WITHOUT ZIPPER)

1. Seam the ends of the boxing together to make a circular piece (see illustration 238).

2. On one side of the circular boxing strip make self-cording by turning enough material over the cord to make sewing easy (see illustration 239).

238. Strip for boxing.

239. Making a welting cord.

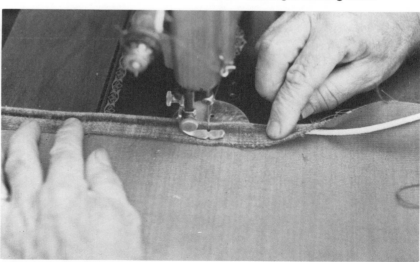

3. Make self-cording on the other side with the same measurement between cording seams all the way around the boxing, using a paper guide (l) or ruler (see illustration 240).

240. Making cushion boxing.

4. On the boxing, in front, put a midpoint chalk mark (m), making sure the pattern on the facing and boxing matches. Mark the front corners (n), then back corners (o) (see illustration 241). On T- or L-form cushions, mark all corners. On oval or rounded forms, mark front, back, and side midpoints. Now you are ready to sew the casing.

241. Marked cushion boxing.

BOXING WITH A ZIPPER

If the cushion is a rectangular form, it is better to make the boxing without a zipper so that it can be reversed on the seat for even wear.

For nonrectangular forms, it is best to install a zipper in the boxing, called a zipper boxing. It is placed in a spot where it will not be seen, usually in the center of the back of the cushion boxing. The longer the zipper opening, the easier it will be to put the cushion in, or remove it from the casing.

Installing the Zipper

1. Measure the total length of the boxing, in this example 98″ (see illustration 242).

2. Subtract the length of the zipper boxing. In this example it is 28″, which leaves 70″ remainder of boxing when subtracted from the total boxing 98″ (TBX minus ZBX=RBX).

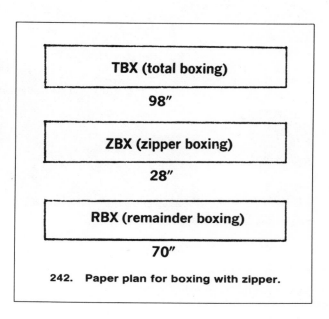

TBX (total boxing)
98″

ZBX (zipper boxing)
28″

RBX (remainder boxing)
70″

242.   Paper plan for boxing with zipper.

3. Cut a strip of material as long as you plan to have the zipper boxing, adding 1″ on each end for the seams, and as wide as needed for the thickness of the cushion. Remember to add 1 1/4″ on top and bottom for self-cording and 1″ for zipper seams.

4. Cut this strip in half lengthwise, leaving an uncut portion 1″ to 2″ to the end so that when installing the zipper the pattern on these two pieces will match (see illustration 243).

243.   Zipper boxing strip.

5. Sew one side of the strip to the zipper starting at the loose (open) end of the zipper as in illustration 244.

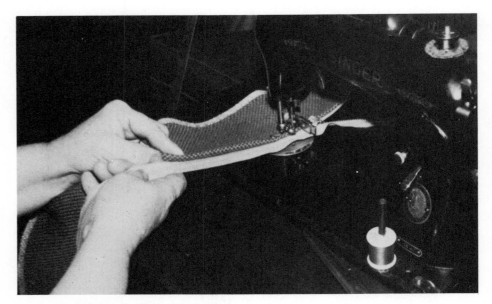

244.   Sewing the zipper to the boxing.

6. Sew the other side close to the first so that the zipper will be invisible as in illustration 245.

245.   Finishing sewing the zipper to the boxing.

7.   Turn inside out and sew the loose sides of the zipper cloth to the fabric to make strong seams and so the loose material will not catch in the zipper (see illustration 246).

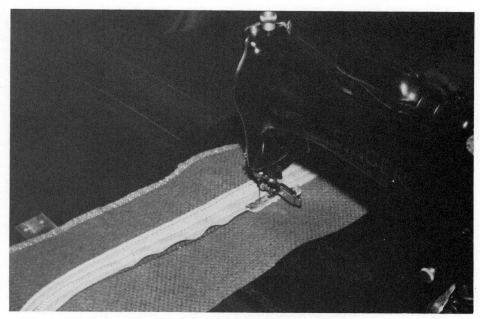

246.   Sewing the loose side of the zipper cloth to the fabric.

8.   Sew the zipper boxing to the remainder of the boxing to give you one complete boxing, with a zipper, needed for your cushion (see illustration 247).

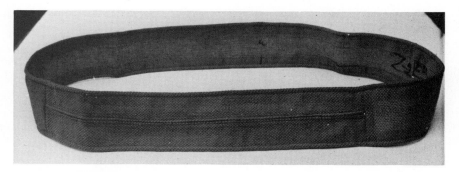

247.   Boxing with a zipper.

Sewing the Boxing to the Facings

To sew the boxing and facings together, always start from the front midpoint marks of the boxing and facings.

1. Under the presser foot of the sewing machine lay a facing (p), finish side up. On top of the facing lay a boxing (q), also finish side up.

2. Join front midpoint marks of the facing (r) and boxing (s), then start with narrow stitches to sew the boxing to the facing so that the seam of the cording lies directly on the sewing chalk mark of the facing (t) (see illustration 248).

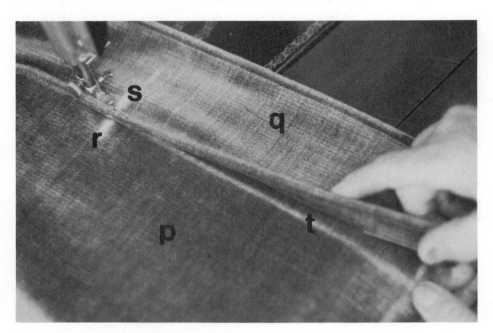

248. Sewing the boxing to cushion facing.

3. As you come to a front-corner mark on the boxing, go 1/8″ over the mark and turn a corner 90 degrees. You will then have a square corner.

Note: Use boxing as a guide for turning corners, since the facing may possibly stretch and give a larger measurement than is needed.

To turn a corner, the machine should be stopped while the needle is in the material you are sewing. Lift the presser foot and turn the material in the direction you wish, while the needle acts as the axis. Lower the presser foot and start to sew.

4. After you have turned the front corner, finish sewing the side, and after turning the back corner, sew the back side about 3″, then stop. On the T- or L-form cushions, turn the front corner, then all T corners, and then the back corner as above.

5. Move the zipper-foot attachment to the other side. Complete the other side the same way as the first one except here you will be sewing in the opposite direction.

6. After turning the second back corner, line up the back sides of the boxing and facing, then complete sewing the back side.

7. In case the back side of the boxing (u) is longer than the back side of the facing (v), as in illustration 249, recheck the measurements of both sides; if both sides have the same measurements, reopen both back corners and move them a little to the back. If both side measurements are not the same, reopen just one corner on the shorter side and move this corner a little to the back. Now line up the sides of the boxing and facing and finish sewing them together. If the back side of the boxing (u) is shorter than the back side of the facing (v), move the corner or corners to the front.

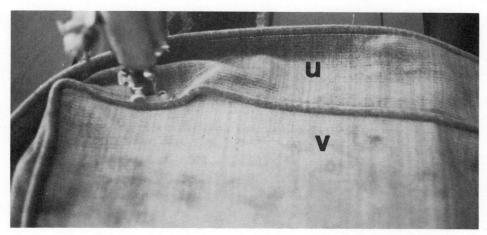

249.

8. Complete the other side of the cushion casing the same way as the first one but:
a) If the cushion is foam rubber, then turn both back corners (w), leaving the back side (x) open as in illustration 250. Put the cushion in and finish sewing this side (y) by hand using a blind stitch (see illustration 251). Pin the side before blindstitching. Use a straight sewing needle, matching color of thread to fabric.

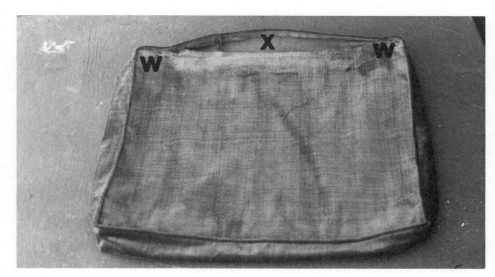

250.

b) If the cushion is innerspring, sew the front completely and halfway down the sides with your sewing machine. After installing the cushion, finish the sides and back of the casing by hand (blind stitching).

c) If the boxing has a zipper, complete all sides on top and bottom of the casing by using a sewing machine.

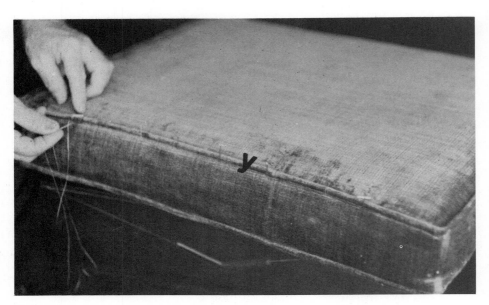

251.

Three-Sided Boxed Cushion

A three-sided boxed cushion is used on the seat of a platform rocker and on a platform chair to match the rocker. The casing is made with boxing on the sides and in the back of the cushion casing. In the front of the casing, do not use welt cording or seam, as it will not be smooth. Prolonged rocking will irritate the legs if cording or a seam is used in front. Also welt cording will wear out fast. Thus, on most movable seats of chairs, cording or the seam in front of the seat is eliminated, for example, on recliners, swivel chairs, etc.

252. Three-sided boxed cushion.

The casing for a three-sided boxed cushion consists of two pieces: facing and boxing.

I. Facing

Use measurements from an old cushion casing (see illustration 252).

1. Measure from the back-cording seam (a) on one side of the cushion to the back-cording seam on the other side (b). In the illustration this measurement is 49″.

2. Measure the width of the cushion in the back from corner (c) to corner (d) and also in the front of the cushion from cording seam (c) to cording seam (d). Width measurement is 21″.

Note: The top and bottom of the cushion facing is made from one piece; select a fabric that has a pattern with no distinguishing top and bottom so that both sides of the cushion can be used.

Measurements from the Seat of the Chair

See illustration 255. When the old cushion is missing or torn, take the cushion casing measurements from the seat of the chair.

1. Measure between the sides of the seat railings (g) and (h) of the chair, in front and in back, between railings (k) and (m). If the dimensions are different in the front and back of the seat, the paper plan will look like illustration 253. Thus, the back of the cushion is narrower than the front.

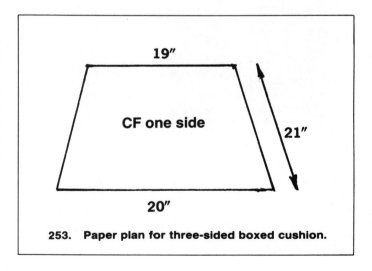

253.   Paper plan for three-sided boxed cushion.

2. Measure from the front-seat railing (n) to the back-seat railing (p). Double this dimension for both sides of the cushion cover. Now add the dimension for the thickness of the cushion. (Remember 1/16″ less for each inch of thickness for a tight fit.) For example, front to back is 21″, double will be 42″, plus 3 3/4″ for cushion of 4″ thickness. Total is 45 3/4″. Add 1″ on all sides for seams.

3. On the finishing side of the fabric, mark the cutting lines in chalk, as per dimensions, and cut facing out (see illustration 254).

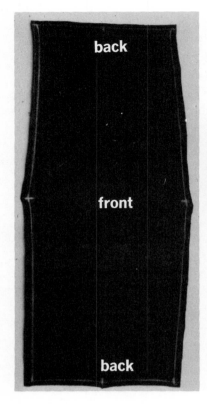

254. Facing for three-sided boxed cushion.

255. Seat of platform chair.

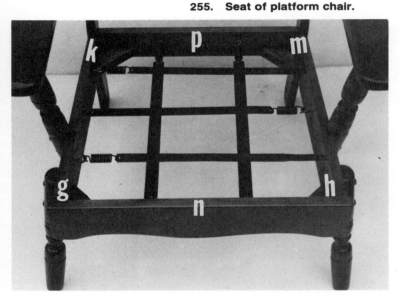

II. Boxing

1. See illustration 252. Measure the length of the boxing from the right front edge of the cushion casing at the cording seam (e) down the side (f), along the back (a), and along the left side of the cushion (g) to the front edge of the cushion casing at the cording seam (h). This total length will give you the total length of the boxing. Add to each end 1 1/4″ for self-cording.

2. Measure the boxing width between the cording seams. Add 1 1/4″ to each side for self-cording.

3. Cut out the boxing as per your dimensions taken in steps 1 and 2.

256. Marking chalk lines for rounded corners.

4. Make self-cording all around the boxing, after making the corners rounded by using a circle with diameter equal to the cushion thickness, making a half circle on both ends of the boxing as in illustration 256.

5. See illustration 257. Make midpoint marks (m) on both ends of the boxing and marks for the back corners (c). The marks (c) are made by folding the boxing in half, the long way, to give a midpoint. Then make measurements in both directions, from the midpoint, a distance equal to half the back cushion dimension.

257. Marked boxing.

Sewing the Casing

To sew the boxing and facing together, always start at the end midpoint marks of the boxing and front (center) midpoint marks of the facing.

1. Under the presser foot of the sewing machine, lay the facing (p) finish side up. Lay the boxing (r) on top of the facing, also finish side up.

2. Join the front midpoint marks of the facing and boxing, then start to sew the boxing to the facing so that the seam of the cording lies directly on the sewing chalk line of the facing (see illustration 258).

258. Sewing the boxing to the facing.

259. The boxing and facing sewed along the side to 3″ around the back corner.

260. Finish sewing the back side of the cushion casing.

3. As you come to the back corner mark on the boxing, go 1/8″ over the mark and turn a corner 90 degrees to give you a square corner. Always use the boxing as a guide for turning corners as the facing can stretch. Sew about 3″ along the back edge and stop (see illustration 259).

4. Move the zipper-foot attachment to the other side, and after lining up the midpoint marks on the facing and boxing, on the other end, proceed as above in the opposite direction.

5. After turning the second back corner, line up the back sides of the boxing and facing and complete sewing the back side (see illustration 260).

6. Complete the other side of the casing the same way as the first one but leave the back side open for installing the cushion, then sew by hand using blind stitching.

Note: For an innerspring cushion, leave about one-third of each side and the back unsewn to install the innerspring cushion, and finish by hand sewing (see illustration 261). If the boxing has a zipper, complete all sides on top and bottom of the casing by using a sewing machine.

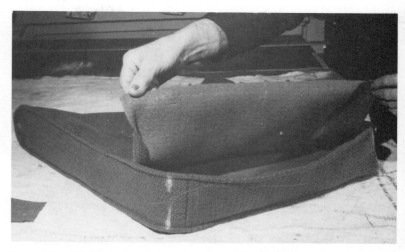

261. The casing is ready for inserting the cushion.

Pillow-Type Cushion

Loose pillow-type cushions are used for the back of platform chairs and attached to the back frame of colonial-style furniture (see illustrations 262 and 263).

To make a pillow-type casing, you must have two facings and a welting cord.

I. Facings

1. See illustration 262. Measure between sides of cording seams (a and b). For example, 24″ as on paper plan. Add 1″ allowance on each side for seams.

263. Pillow-type cushion attached to the back of the chair.

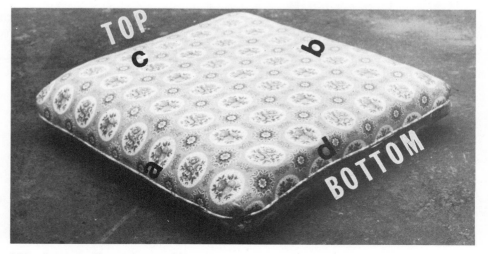

262. Loose pillow-type cushion.

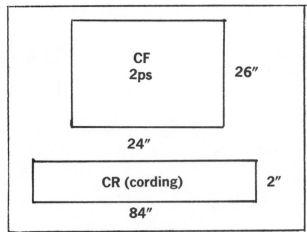

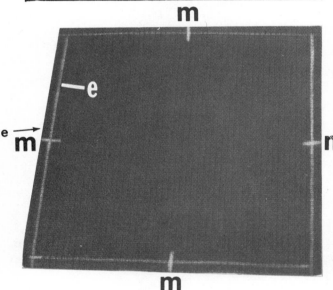

2. Measure between top (c) and bottom (d) of the cording seams. For example, 26″ as on paper plan. Add 1″ allowance on each side for seams.

264. Paper plan for pillow-type cushion.

3. On the finishing side of the upholstery fabric, mark chalk lines for the two facings 24″ x 26″, which will be the sewing lines (e). Mark a 1″ seam allowance around the outside of the sewing line to mark your cutting line. On each side of the facing, mark midpoint mark (m) and cut out piece as in illustration 265.

265. Facing for pillow-type cushion.

II. Welting Cord

1. Measure the welting cord all around the cushion as in illustration 266. For example, 84″. Put on the paper plan.

2. Cut a 2″-wide strip as long as needed, and give 2″ allowance for the seam. In this case it is 84″ exactly, plus 2″ allowance for the seam, which is 86″ to cut.

266. Taking measurements for welting cord.

2. Cut a 2"-wide strip as long as needed, and give 2" allowance for the seam. In this case it is 84" exactly, plus 2" allowance for the seam, which is 86" to cut.

3. Seam both ends of the strip, then make the welting cord; it will be a circular one. Mark all four corners (c) and put midpoint marks (m) on each side (see illustration 267).

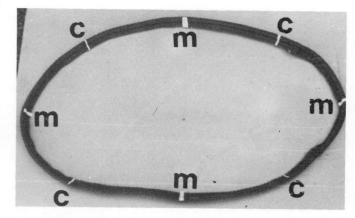

267. Marked corners (c) and midpoints (m) for the sides.

III. Sewing the Welting Cord and Facings Together

1. See illustration 268. Under the presser foot of the sewing machine, lay a facing (f), finish side up. On top of the facing lay a welting cord (g) so that the cording will lie to the inside.

2. Join top midpoint marks (m) of the facing and welting cord. Then start, with narrow stitches, to sew the welting cord to the facing so that the stitching is on the wrong side of the material.

268. Sewing the cording to the facing.

3. Using the welting cord as a guide for the corners, start to sew at the top midpoint mark and stop on the corner. Go in one direction from the midpoint marks (m) to the corners (c) and on each corner stop. Finish sewing the cording to the facing in one direction from the midpoint marks to the corners as in illustration 269.

269. Cording is sewed to the facing from midpoint marks to the corners in one direction only.

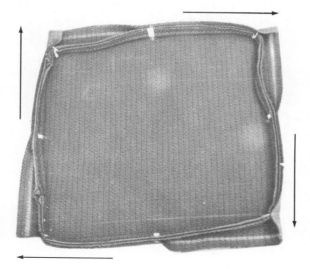

4. Move the zipper-foot attachment to the other side and start to sew from the midpoint marks (m) to the corners (c) in the opposite direction. Now all four corners (c) on the facing will fold evenly by themselves as in illustration 270.

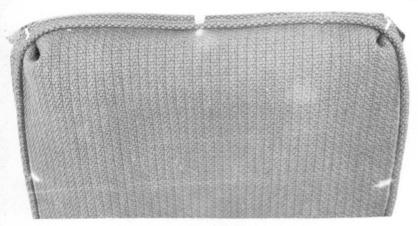

270. The cording sewed to the facing.

5. Sew the corners inside out as in illustration 271 and cut off excess material as in illustration 272.

271. Sewing a corner.

272. Cutting off excess material.

6. Sew the cording to the facing at the corners, sewing about 2″ along the seam to secure the cording at the corners to the facing (see illustration 273).

7. To complete the other side of the cushion casing, you must attach the top facing with the cording, which you have just finished, to the bottom facing, finish side to finish side, and sew the same way as before from midpoint marks to the corners and finish the corners as in steps 5 and 6.

273. Sewing the cording to the facing at the corner.

If the cushion is foam rubber, then leave the bottom side open. Put the cushion in and finish sewing this side by hand, using a blind stitch.

If the cushion is innerspring, sew the top completely and halfway down the sides with your sewing machine. After installing the cushion, finish the sides and the bottom of the casing by hand, using a blind stitch.

Step 14

INSTALLING THE WELTING CORD

Welting cord is used to give a tailored appearance to an upholstered piece and for hiding stitches where covers must be blindstitched. Single welt may be installed on many places on a piece of furniture: the bottom of a chair or sofa, on the arm panels, and on the outside back edges. Some parts of the welt can be tacked to the frame without tacking tape but other parts need tacking tape. Now we will install the welt on the outside back top edge, with outside wing edges, of a wing chair.

1. Make welting cord as long as needed for your project.

2. See illustration 274. Start at the bottom of one wing post (a) and tack one end of the welt to the bottom of the arm rail; following the outside edge of the wing post, tack the welt, without tacking tape, to the wing edge from the bottom (a) to the top (c), using staples or tacks.

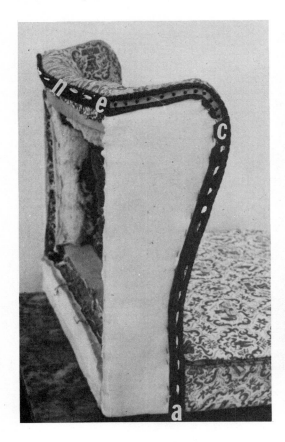

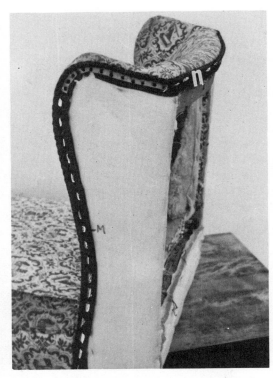

274. Installed cording on the outside wings and the back.

3. Tack the welt to the outside edge of the wing top rail from the front (c) to the back (e), using tacking tape and tacks. On the curves, force the tacking tape to follow the edge.

4. Tack the welt to the outside edge of the top back rail (n) without tacking tape, using staples or tacks.

5. Install the welt on the other wing in the same way as on the first one.

Note: On edges where welt is installed without tacking tape, install the final cover, using blind tacking, with tacking tape. On edges where welt is installed with tacking tape, install the final cover, using blind stitching.

For fitting welting cord on the curved edges and the corners, see illustration 275.

1. If the edge is curved to the inside (d), you should snip cut the cording excess.

2. If the edge is curved to the outside (g), you should cut "V's" in the cording excess.

3. On the inside corner of the edge (r), you should snip cut the cording excess.

4. On the outside corner of the edge (k), you should cut a "V" in the cording excess.

275. Fitting the welting cord.

Step 15

OUTSIDE WINGS

After you have completed the inside of your project, you will start to cover the outside. If there are wings, you must cover the outside of the wings before covering any other parts of your project.

1. Take measurements of the outside wing for the final cover, widest points, as in illustration 276. Add 1 1/2″ to each side for handling.

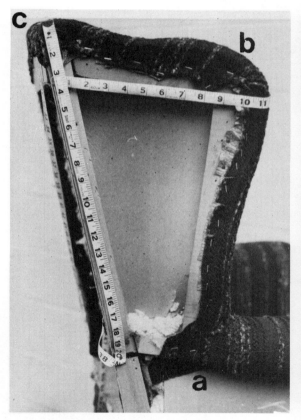

| 276. Outside wing measurements. | 277. Cording is installed. |

2. Cut two pieces of fabric as per measurements and matching in pattern for the left and right wings.

3. See illustration 276. Make welting cord as long as the measurement of the outside edge of the wing, from the bottom of the arm rail (a) to the top (b), continue to the back (c), add the length of the top back rail and the outside edge of the other wing all the way to the bottom of the arm rail on the other side. This cording will be one piece for both wings and back.

4. See illustration 277. Install the cording so that the seam of the cording lies on the wooden edge. On top of the wing edge, install the cording with tacking tape and firmly tack to the wood edge. On front of the wing edge, tack the cording without tacking tape. Here you will install the final cover with blind tacking, but on top you will use blind stitching. Sew the top of the wing cover with a straight sewing needle, directly to the seam of the cording. If the top edge of the wing is not curved, blind-tack the top edge and blindstitch the front edge as in illustration 278. This is the outside wing cover for the piped-back wing chair on page 51, illustration 92.

278. Blind-tacking the outside wing cover at the top.

5. Fill up the hollow part of the wing with cotton or foam and cover with muslin (see illustration 279).

6. See illustration 280. Place the wing cover on the outside of the wing, trace the top and the front edge of the wing. On the side where it will be blind-tacked, put a mark (m) on the wing cover and on the edge of the wing so that you can line the pieces up when blind tacking.

7. Cut along line (d), leaving 1/2" allowance for blind tacking and stitching.

279. Filled outside wing covered with muslin.   **280. Marked outside wing cover for cutting.**

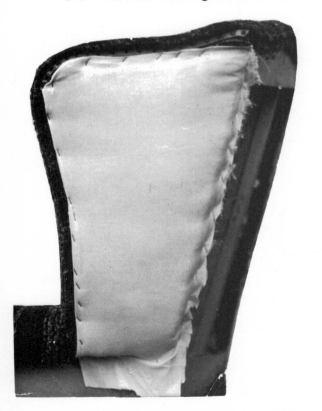

8. Place the outside wing cover inside out so that marks (m) line up and blind-tack the front side of the wing cover as in illustration 281.

9. Pull the cover over the wing. Tack the bottom of the wing cover to the bottom of the arm rail, and the back side of the wing cover to the back post. Tack the edge of the top, folded underneath, temporarily as in illustration 282. Blindstitch the top of the wing cover to the cording seam. Remove the tacks to complete.

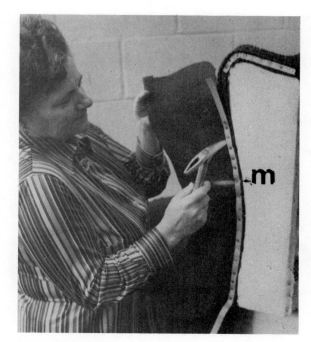

281.   Blind-tacking the outside wing cover.

282.   Wing ready for blind-stitching.

283.   Blind-stitching the top of the outside wing cover.

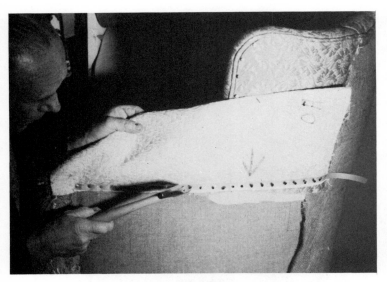

284.   Blind-tacking the top of the outside arm cover.

Step 16

OUTSIDE ARMS

On some furniture styles the front of the arms are completed first before installing the outside arm covers. The front of the arms will be explained in step 17. On other styles, however, the outside of the arms is done before the front. The outside arm extends from the top arm rail to the bottom of the project and from the front arm post to the back post. All four sides of the final cover are tacked to the frame. On most styles of chairs and sofas the top of the final cover is blind-tacked to the arm rail, using tacking tape, as in illustration 284. The front of the cover is blind-tacked to the arm post, using a metal tacking strip, as in illustration 285. We are installing the outside arm cover for a piped-back wing chair, which we started on page 51.

285.   Blind-tacking the front of the outside arm cover.

The bottom of the cover is tacked to the bottom of the seat rail. The back of the cover is tacked to the back post. The outside arm covers will be finished differently, depending on the arm style. When taking measurements for the final cover, use the widest points only. Illustration 286 shows the measurements for the outside arm cover. Add a total of 3″ for handling.

286. Taking measurements for the outside arm cover.

Here are some finished outside arms:

The back and bottom for most styles are installed the same way. The back is tacked to the back post (outside) and the bottom of the cover is tacked to the bottom of the side seat rail.

287. The top of this cover is blind-tacked with tacking tape. The front is blind-tacked with a metal tacking strip.

288. The top of this cover is blind-tacked with tacking tape and the front is tacked to the front arm post.

289. The top of this cover is blind-tacked with tacking tape and the front is finished with upholstery nails.

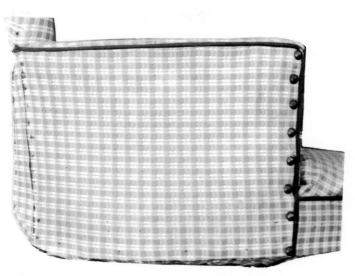

290. Cording is installed first on the top and front. The top of this cover is blind-tacked with tacking tape and the front is finished with upholstery nails.

291. The top of this cover is blind-tacked with tacking tape and the front is finished with double cording.

292. Edges are finished off with double cording.

Step 17

FRONT ARMS

The front arm is made and finished differently, depending on the style of the arm.

I. Front Arms Made of Wood

On some chairs the front arm is made of wood. In this case the unfinished edges are finished off with gimp or nail trim on old-fashioned pieces and with double cording on modern styles as in illustration 292.

To apply gimp, double cording, and nail trim, see pages 65–67.

II. Front Arms with Arm Panels

See illustrations 293 and 294. Many types of arms are made so that the inside and outside arm covers are tacked in front of the arm as in illustration 294. In this case the unfinished front arms are finished with arm panels, which are made in different forms. Arm panels can be made of wood and finished in the desired color (wooden panels).

Plywood or Heavy Cardboard Slightly Padded and Covered with Fabric

Other types of panels are called covered arm panels. Some are covered without cording (b), others are covered with cording (c). Cording is installed to the covered panel (see illustration 295).

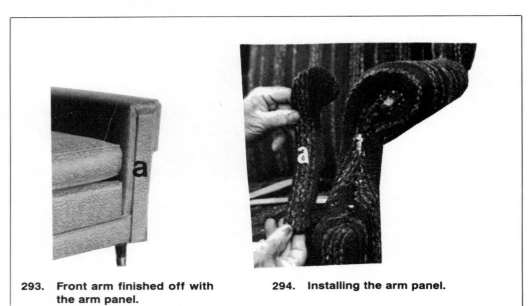

293. Front arm finished off with the arm panel.

294. Installing the arm panel.

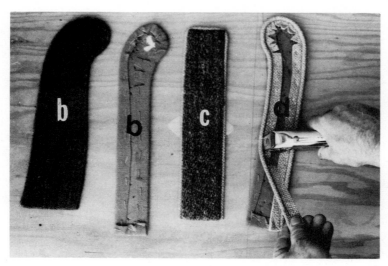

295. Arm panels.

To install the panel to the front arm, use carpenter finishing nails. The length depends upon the thickness of the arm panel with padding on the front arm. Usually sizes from 3/4″ to 1 1/4″ are good for this job. About five to ten nails are enough to install the arm panel. Hammer in the nail through the arm panel and into the front arm post. As soon as the head of the nail comes close to the surface of the fabric, pull the fabric over the head with a curved needle as in illustration 296, then completely hammer in the nail. Pulling the fabric over the head of the nail avoids breaking the weaving threads.

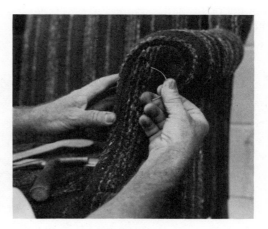

296. Pulling the fabric over the nail-head, using a curved needle.

III. Boxed Front Arms

For details on closed boxed arms, see "Closed Boxed Arms," pages 86–88. The arm boxing is installed for both the top of the arm (e) and the front of the arm (g) in one piece (see illustration 297).

IV. Smooth Finished Front Arms

For a smooth finished front arm, see illustration 178, page 83.

V. Front Arms Finished with an Inside Arm Cover

For a front arm finished with an inside arm cover, see illustration 167, page 79.

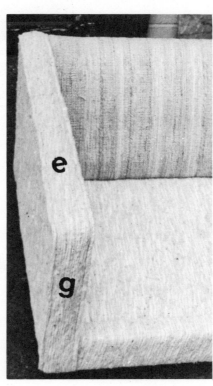

297. Boxed front arm (g).

Step 18

OUTSIDE BACK

The outside back on most pieces of furniture extends between the back posts and from the top back rail to the bottom of the chair or sofa.

The outside back installations:

1. Measure the outside back, widest points only, between the back posts and between the top back rail and the bottom of the chair or sofa. Add 1 1/2″ to each side of your measurements.

2. Cut in rectangular form the outside back cover according to the measurements. Be sure to center the pattern.

3. Mark midpoint marks on the top and bottom of the back cover, and on the top and bottom of the back of your project.

4. Blind-tack the top of the back cover to the top back rail.

a) On straightlined tops of backs, line up top midpoint marks, then blind-tack, using tacking tape.

b) On curved tops of backs, before tacking you must trim the top of the back cover according to the form of the top back rail. Illustration 298 shows chalk marking on the top of the back cover, following the top edge. Cut off excess (x) on the line and blind-tack as in illustration 299.

We are installing the back cover for the piped-back wing chair, which we started on page 51, illustration 92.

298. Marking the top of the back cover.

299. Blind-tacking the top of the back cover.

Note: On very curved tops as on this back, it is very difficult to blind-tack the whole top. In this case blind-tack the middle part halfway and blindstitch the rest.

5. Blind-tack the sides of the back cover to the back posts, using a metal tacking strip.

6. Tack the bottom of the back cover to the bottom of the back seat rail.

Illustrations 300 and 301 show the piped-back wing chair completed, which was started on page 51.

300. Piped-back wing chair (side view).

301. Piped-back wing chair (front view).

302. The welting cord installed to the bottom outside edges of the seat rails.

Step 19

THE BOTTOM

When your piece is completely upholstered, except for a skirt, if you wish to put one on, turn it upside down and start working on the bottom of your project. If welting cord is to be used along the bottom edge as in illustration 302, install the welt to the bottom outside edges of the seat rails, using tacking tape for firm finishing. Then cut a piece of cambric 2″ larger than the bottom of the seat. Tack the cambric over the entire bottom. All the edges of the cover should be folded under for a smooth finish. Start tacking the cambric in the center of each side and go to the corners. Cut openings for the legs as in illustrations 120 and 121 on page 63. The finished bottom will look like illustration 303.

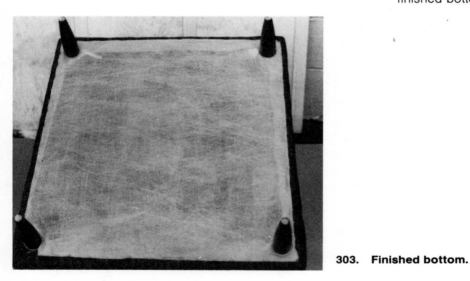

303. Finished bottom.

Step 20

THE SKIRT

A chair or sofa looks much more modern and finished with a skirt around it. It not only beautifies a piece of furniture but also tells you the style. Early American or colonial styles almost always require the box-pleated skirt, thus the term early American or colonial. Modern furniture uses the kick-box skirt.

Box-Pleated Skirt:

The amount of material needed depends on what kind of pleating one is going to use. The open type of box pleat requires less material because there is space between the pleats.

For a chair you need approximately one yard of material.

Open pleats look better than the closed type.

The height of the skirt should be measured from the bottom of the seat rail to 1″ from the floor (see illustration 306); add 2″ for tacking and a hem.

The total length of the material for the skirt is approximately two and a half times the length around the base of the seat rails. For example, if the measurement around the chair is 120″, you need approximately 300″ length of material. I will illustrate the 3″ pleats with a 2″ space between pleats. A box-pleated skirt consists of two pieces: welting cord and skirting.

304. Closed box-pleated skirt.

305. Open box-pleated skirt.

306. Measurement for height of the skirt.

Welting Cord:

1. Measure around the bottom of the chair or sofa as in illustration 307.

307. Measurement for the length of the skirt.

2. Cut a 2″ wide strip of the upholstery material as long as the measurement and add 2″ allowance for a seam at the ends.

3. Sew the ends together (seam together), making one circular piece.

4. Make welting cord from this circular strip. The finished cording will look like the cording for a pillow-type cushion (see illustration 267, page 129).

5. Put welting on the chair around the seat railing and mark the corners and the front on the cording (see illustration 308).

6. Take the marked cording off your chair. This is your prepared welting cord.

308.   Marked cording.

Skirting:

1. Cut the pieces of upholstery material the length and width of your project, including allowance. Here you will need to sew several pieces together so that all pieces of the pattern are upright.

2. Finish the bottom by sewing a 1/4″ hem (see illustration 309). On the top (1) of the finishing side of the skirting strip at a distance from the hem (2) of your exact skirt height, draw a chalk line (3). You will use this line for sewing the welting cord after the skirting is pleated.

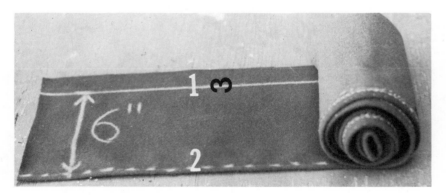

309.   Marked skirting
(6″ exact skirt height).

3. No matter what kind of pleating you are doing, each corner must have closed pleats (see illustration 305). Thus, you will always have a pleat on each side of the corner, and each side will always have one less space (between pleats) than pleats. For example, one side with six pleats will have five spaces between pleats. The dimensions of the sides will determine the amount of pleats needed. You can change dimensions of the pleats by a small amount (for fitting) and not be able to notice the difference from one side to the other. If we are making a skirt with 3″ pleats and 2″ spaces between pleats, and the side measures 23″, how many pleats will we need? Since one pleat (3″) and one space (2″) total 5″, if we have five of each, that would be 25″, but we have one less space (2″) so that we have five pleats (3″ each) and four spaces (2″ each) for a total of 23″, which is perfect. However, if one side was 24″, we could make the pleats (five of them) equally larger.

Pleating:

Start pleating from the back right corner of your chair. Use a guiding marker with two marks, as in illustration 310, one for pleat width (3″) and one for space width (2″).

1. See illustration 311. Leave about one yard of skirting material (b) for the back of the chair and then make 3″ closed pleats (c) for the corner. Press each pleat with a damp cloth and pin it with two pins on the top and bottom as in illustration 312.

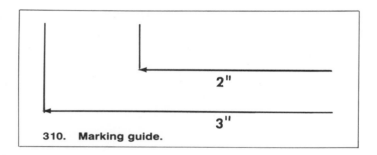

2"

3"

310. Marking guide.

311. Closed pleats for the corner.

312. Pressing the pleats.

2. Using the marking guide, mark on the top and bottom a 2″ space from the edge (d) (see illustration 313). Then fold your next pleat (e) so that its edge (f) is at the chalk marks (see illustration 314).

3. Measure 3″ with the marking guide, from the edge (f) of the pleat (e) (illustration 315) on the top and bottom and fold on the marks as in illustration 316.

313.   Marking the space between pleats.

4. Repeat for all the pleats, pressing and pinning them.

314.   Folding a pleat.

315.   Marking the pleat.

316.   Folding the pleat.

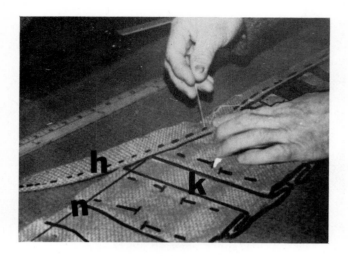

5. See illustrations 317 and 318. After you have finished the pleating for one side of the chair, sew the welting cord (h) to the skirting (k). Use the corner marks (m) on the cording to line up with the center of the closed pleats and sew along the skirting line (n). Continue for the remaining sides as above until finished.

317. Sewing the cording to the skirting.

318. Skirt for one side of the chair completed.

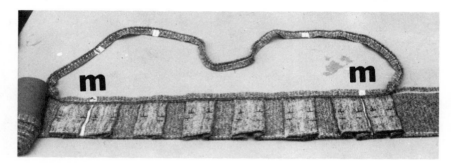

The completed skirt will look like the one in illustration 319.

319. Completed skirt for a chair.

6. Fold the cording down under the pleats and press down the pleats as in illustration 310.

320.   Final pressing the pleats down.

7. Put the chair upside down on your workbench. Using a tacking tape and tacks #8 or #10, depending on the thickness of material, blind-tack the skirt to the frame as in illustration 321. Make sure that the cording is installed straight and the skirt is the same height from the floor on each side.

321.   Blind tacking the skirt.

8. Put your chair right side up and pull the skirt down. The completely installed skirt is shown in illustration 322.

322. Installed skirt.

323. Kick-box skirt on the sofa.

The Kick-Box Skirt:

The kick-box skirt is used on modern furniture. It requires much less material than the pleated skirt. It also consists of cording and skirting.

1. Measure around the bottom of the chair or sofa the same way as you did for the pleated skirt (see illustration 307, page 146).

2. Complete the welting cord the same way as you did for the pleated skirt (see steps #2, #3, and #4, page 146).

3. See illustration 324. Install the cording to the seat railing in position at the planned height.

a) Tack the cording on sides (a) of each corner. The height of each corner must be the same from the floor.

b) See illustration 325. Lay a yardstick or straight board along the top surface of the cording. Using the edge of the yardstick as a guide for making the cording straight, tack or staple the cording to the frame. Space the tacks or staples about 3″ or 4″ apart. Do the other sides similarly.

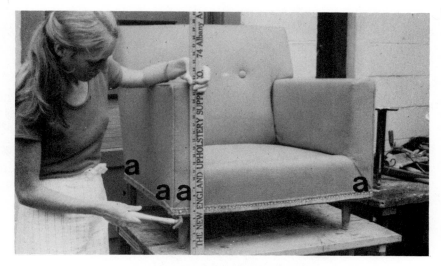

324. Installing the cording.

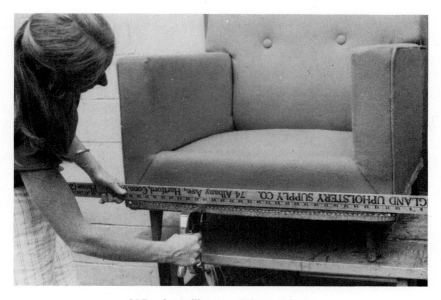

325. Installing straight cording.

Skirting:

1. For a chair, measure each side of the seat railing, from corner to corner (four sides). For a sofa, measure the sides and back, corner to corner. In the front, measure from the corners and the cushion joints as in illustration 323.

2. Cut a piece for each side of the planned skirt height plus 2″ allowance for hem and blind tacking, and as long as needed with 2″ allowance for finishing the ends. Also cut four narrow pieces for the corners about 8″ wide and of the same height as for the sides. For a sofa cut narrow pieces for each corner and cushion joint.

3. Hem the sides and bottom of each piece. Hem the long pieces to fit exactly from corner to corner. The finished pieces for each side and for the corners of the chair are shown in illustration 326.

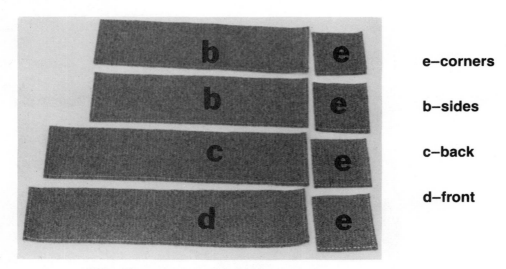

e–corners

b–sides

c–back

d–front

326.   Completed pieces of the skirting.

4. On the top of the wrong side of each long piece at a distance from the hem of your exact skirt height, draw a line as in illustration 327. You will use this line for blind tacking. On the corner pieces the marking line must be 1/4″ lower than on the long pieces. After folding over the narrow pieces, the long pieces are folded over the narrow pieces and the hemline will be the same height from the floor.

327.   Line for blind-tacking.

5. Attach each piece in place as in illustration 328, so that the marking line is close to the cording. Then blind-tack as in illustration 329. The completely installed kick-box skirt for the chair is shown in illustration 330 and for the sofa in illustration 323, page 152.

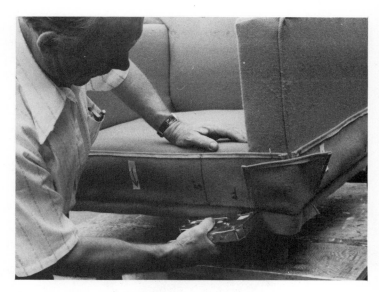

328.   Attaching the kick-box skirt.

329.   Blind-tacking the skirt.

330.   Installed kick-box skirt.

The Gathered or Shirred Skirt:

A gathered skirt requires half the amount of material as a pleated skirt and is made from light fabric. A skirt is made by feeding the material into the machine in uniform bunches, causing it to wrinkle in front of the foot on the sewing machine.

1. Cut pieces of your fabric for skirting about one and a half times as long as the measurement around your chair. Be sure all pieces are cut out in the same direction.

2. Sew all pieces together in the same direction into one long strip, and then hem on the bottom.

3. Sew down the gathers, on top of the skirting, 1/2″ from the edge.

4. Sew cording over the gathered top, facing down.

5. Blind-tack in place the same way as a pleated skirt.

331.   Gathered skirt.

Step 21

ARM CAPS

Arm caps are a very useful addition to your furniture. They help prevent the arms from wearing out or make a used piece look better. Your leftover material can be put to use for this purpose or you may use any suitable matching material that fits your decor.

A.   Rounded Top of the Arm:

Cap for rounded top arm consists of two pieces sewn together.

1.   Measure the depth of the arm from the front top edge to the back of the chair as in illustration 332.

2.   Measure the width from the middle of the cushion boxing to the outside arm (4″ from the top) as in illustration 333.

332.   Measuring depth of the arm.
333.   Taking a measurement for the arm cap.

3.   Cut, from your upholstery fabric, two matching pieces in dimension and pattern, one for the left arm and one for the right arm.

4.   Cut two matching pieces (for two arms) about 1″ larger than the width of the arm and 5″ from the bottom to top.

5. Put the small piece, inside out, on the arm and trace the edge as in illustration 334. This is the sewing line.

334. Tracing the edge of the arm.

6. Cut about 1″ excess material from the outside of the sewing line.

7. Follow the chalk line. Sew this small piece to the large one, both inside out (on the wrong side).

8. Make a hem on each side.

Note: Prepare the right arm cap inside out on the left arm. Also prepare similarly the left arm cap inside out on the right arm. For the finishing arm cap, see illustration 335.

335. Finished cap for rounded arm top.

B. Rectangular Form of the Arm:

Cap for rectangular form is made from one piece.

1. See illustration 336. Measure (a) to (b), 4″ always. Add top from (b) to (c) and (c) to (d). In this example the total is 16″.

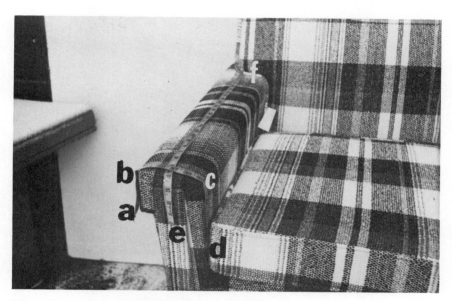

336. Taking measurements for the arm cap.

2. Measure from the back of the chair (f) to the front arm edge (line b-c), and add 4″ to point (e). In this example it is 27″.

3. Cut two matching pieces in dimension and pattern for the arms. In this example it is 16″ x 27″.

4. See illustration 337. Draw a line a-b-c-d 4″ from border (e). Along this line measure a-b (always 4″). From b to c is the dimension for the top of your arm (5″ in this example). From c to d is the remainder (7″ in this example). The lines a-b-e and e-c-d are the sewing lines. Make cutting lines 1″ from the sewing lines and cut out excess material (x).

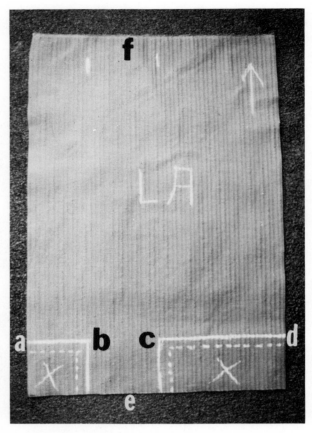

337. Marked fabric for the arm cap.

5. See illustration 338. Sew lines (a) and (b) together and lines (c) and (d) together, inside out as marked.

6. Make a hem on all sides. The finished arm cap is shown in illustration 339.

338.   The arm cap ready for sewing.

339.   Finished cap for rectangular form arm top.

Remember, as I have already stated in the beginning of the book, anyone can do an outstanding job of reupholstery. I have given you all the knowledge that you will need to create a new piece of furniture. Whatever the style, you should have no difficulty in creating a new look to an old or worn piece of furniture. Just follow the step-by-step directions and use the illustrations. Everything has been done to simplify the task at hand. You can create a piece to reflect your own tastes in style and fabric, and save money in the process. All you need is time and this book.

After your project is completed you will feel proud in knowing you did it yourself.

Peter Nesovich

INDEX